W9-CCU-256

THE SHIH TZU

Deborah Wood

The Shih Tzu

Project Team
Editor: Janice Biniok
Copy Editor: Joann Woy
Design: Lundquist Design
Series Design: Mada Design
Series Originator: Dominique De Vito

T.F.H. Publications
President/CEO: Glen S. Axelrod
Executive Vice President: Mark E. Johnson
Publisher: Christopher T. Reggio
Production Manager: Kathy Bontz

T.F.H. Publications, Inc.
One TFH Plaza
Third and Union Avenues
Neptune City, NJ 07753

06 07 08 09 10 1 3 5 7 9 8 6 4 2
Printed and bound in China

Library of Congress Cataloging-in-Publication Data
Wood, Deborah, 1952-
The Shih tzu / Deborah Wood.
p. cm.
Includes index.
ISBN 0-7938-3642-5 (alk. paper)
1. Shih tzu. I. Title.
SF429.S64W66 2006
636.76—dc22

This book has been published with the intent to provide accurate and authoritative information in regard to the subject matter within. While every precaution has been taken in preparation of this book, the author and publisher expressly disclaim responsibility for any errors, omissions, or adverse effects arising from the use or application of the information contained herein. The techniques and suggestions are used at the reader's discretion and are not to be considered a substitute for veterinary care. If you suspect a medical problem consult your veterinarian.

The Leader In Responsible Animal Care For Over 50 Years!™
www.tfh.com

TABLE OF CONTENTS

Chapter 1

HISTORY of the Shih Tzu

Your Shih Tzu comes from a line of small, companion-sized dogs who have been with humans for hundreds, and maybe even thousands, of years. It's no wonder your dog seems to understand your thoughts and moods better than most humans do!

The more we learn about dogs, the more we realize that ours is an ancient friendship. DNA tests suggest dogs may have become separated from wolves sometime between 50,000 and 130,000 years ago—far earlier than originally believed. Cave drawings in India and France, dating back about 25,000 years, depict animals that look like domestic dogs. When we imagine these ancient scenes, we think of people hunting wooly mammoth with the first dogs at their sides.

What's surprising is that lap dogs may not have been all that far behind. Recently unearthed archeological evidence indicates that little dogs resembling the Maltese may have been present in the northern deserts of China as early as 10,000 years ago. It seems that humankind has needed small companion dogs almost as much as herding, hunting, and guarding dogs.

Certainly, small dogs existed in China and Tibet 2,500 years ago. In China, the ancestors of today's Pugs and Pekingese were providing comfort to Chinese royalty. In Tibet, the forebears of Lhasa Apsos, Tibetan Terriers, and Tibetan Spaniels were living with Buddhist monks.

Just where the first Shih Tzu fit into this picture is a matter of heated debate among people who love the breed. Some Shih Tzu breed historians firmly assert that the Shih Tzu is a Chinese breed, completely separate from the Tibetan breeds. Others say that Shih Tzu came directly from the Tibetan monasteries to the Chinese palaces, and that Lhasa Apsos and Shih Tzu are basically variations of the same ancient dog breed.

It's impossible to know the Shih Tzu's exact origins. China has participated in global trade for many hundreds of years. A free flow of religious thought, philosophy, and inventions existed among China, Tibet, and India long before Europe became a civilized region. It seems highly likely that little dogs were a natural part of that free flow of commerce and ideas. Most likely there were many times when the genetics of Chinese

That Name!

Shih Tzu is pronounced "sheedzoo." The name "Shih Tzu" is both plural and singular for the breed—like "deer" or "fish."

and Tibetan dogs influenced the breeding of the dogs in both countries.

Experts now mostly agree that Shih Tzu should be considered a Chinese breed, rather than a Tibetan breed—even if Tibetan influences can be found in Shih Tzu.

THE SHIH TZU IN CHINA

There occurs a delightful merging of art, dogs, and mythology in the lion-dog statues that first appeared in China about 200 BCE. Called *foo dogs*, these statues look like something between a dog and a lion. Most often, they are found in pairs, with a male holding his paw on a ball and a female with a pup. (Some call it a cub.) The foo dog is also sometimes called the "Celestial Dog" or the "Happiness Dog." The animal is a symbol of energy and value. Some historians argue that Chinese artists hadn't ever seen a lion and were trying to (poorly) represent this animal in the foo dog art. That seems to be an underestimation of these artists; it's more likely they were carving exactly what they meant to carve.

Shih Tzu, Pekingese, and Lhasa Apsos (all called at one time or another "lion dogs") have taken credit for being the inspiration for the foo dogs. All have shaggy fur, large chests, and tails held high over their backs, as do the foo dogs. It's impossible to guess whether the temple and palace dogs were

The exact origin of the Shih Tzu is unclear, although his Far Eastern ancestry is certain, and his careful breeding is legendary.

the inspiration for the art, or whether the art led to the selective breeding of dogs who resembled the lion statues. In any event, fierce foo dog statues still protect many temple gates, homes, and estates.

Because the fur that radiates from their faces resembles a flower, Shih Tzu have been called chrysanthemum dogs.

The first "celebrity" owner of a Shih Tzu was the Chinese dowager empress Tzu Hsi, one of the most famous figures in Chinese history. She was born in 1835, and at age 16, became one of Emperor Hsien Feng's many concubines. She was the only woman to bear an heir for the emperor. When the emperor died in 1861, the 5-year-old boy became the new emperor, but the real power behind the throne was China's "dragon lady"—Tzu Hsi. Through many twists and turns, she basically remained in power until she died in 1908.

The dowager empress was notorious for her excesses. She spent untold sums on banquets, jewels, and other luxuries. She

Did You Know?

Shih Tzu are sometimes called "chrysanthemum dogs," because the fur that radiates from their faces resembles the petals of that flower.

Famous Firsts

First American Shih Tzu Champion: Ch. Bjorneholm's Pif

First Shih Tzu to go Best in Show: American and Canadian Ch. Chumulari Ying Ying

First Master Agility Champion: MACH 4 Harper's Naughty Niki CD RN

First Obedience Trial Champion: OTCH Itsy Bitsy Cookie Monster UDX3

served as many as 150 dishes at a single banquet, drank from a jade cup, and ate with golden chopsticks. Her eunuchs may have murdered her enemies (including some of her relatives) at her request. One of her many excessive passions was small dogs, including Pekingese and Shih Tzu. The palace eunuchs cared for and supervised the breeding of more than 100 of these small dogs. An existing photograph of the dowager empress shows her with a dog who is clearly a small, black Shih Tzu. When Tzu Hsi died, the breeding program was dispersed.

THE SHIH TZU IN ENGLAND

Reports exist of British officers receiving gifts of Shih Tzu over the years, but no organized breeding program was undertaken in England until the twentieth century. In 1928, Mona Brownrigg was stationed with her husband in Beijing and there acquired her first Shih Tzu. She later became a driving force behind the breed in England. Her dogs produced their first litter in England in 1930.

Little dogs have been very successful in the show ring.

Shih Tzu quickly became popular with Americans when they were introduced in the 1940s, and they remain so today.

A significant controversy had to be settled before the future of the Shih Tzu could be assured. Shih Tzu with short noses were imported from China. Meanwhile, fanciers were importing "Tibetan Lion Dogs," mostly through India. These dogs were larger, coarser in build, and had heads very different from those of the little lion dogs from China. Originally, both types of dogs were shown under the umbrella of the Apso and Lion Dog Club. However, it became clear the two dogs were very different.

In 1934, the fanciers of the short-nosed dogs separated from the club and adopted the name of Shih Tzu for their dogs. A total of 14 Shih Tzu (seven dogs and seven bitches) were listed with the group and became the foundation of most, if not all, of today's Shih Tzu throughout the world. The Kennel Club (KC) recognized the breed in 1940.World War II, of course, interrupted dog shows. The first two English champion Shih

Tzu got their titles in 1949. Lady Brownrigg owned both. They were Ch. Ta Chi of Taishan and Ch. Yu Mo Chuang of Boydon.

Ironically, 1949 was also the year that Mao Tse-Tung completed his communist revolution in China. It was a fortunate turn of events for the breed that English fanciers had become enamored of the little dogs. The Chinese government, at that time, considered small dogs like Shih Tzu to be decadent. Probably no Shih Tzu survived in China during the dark years of the Chinese Cultural Revolution.

Celebrities and Shih Tzu

Celebrities have embraced little dogs, and Shih Tzu are no exception. Famous Shih Tzu owners include Jane Seymour, Nicole Richie, and Geri Haliwell. Expect to see more Shih Tzu in the arms of the rich and famous as the little-dog trend continues.

THE SHIH TZU IN AMERICA

Americans first saw a significant number of Shih Tzu when servicemen brought them home from Europe after World War II. The American Shih Tzu Club was formed in 1963 and incorporated in 1968, bringing together diverse groups that had supported the breed since the 1950s.

The American Kennel Club (AKC) admitted the dogs to the miscellaneous class in 1955. Some confusion and reported crossbreeding still occurred between Shih Tzu and Lhasa Apsos. The full recognition of the breed was delayed until Shih Tzu fanciers could prove six pure generations of Shih Tzu to the AKC, with no crosses to either Lhasas or Pekingese. The American Shih Tzu Club was able to do so, and the breed was finally recognized by the AKC in 1969.

The breed was instantly successful in the show ring. In fact, a dog who became an American and Canadian champion, Chumulari Ying Ying, won a Best in Show on September 1, 1969—the very first day the breed could compete for AKC championship points! Twelve days later, Bjorneholm's Pif became the first U.S. breed champion. (Pif was Ying-Ying's sire, so a lot of winning was all in the family during those first weeks.)

Since then, the rise of breed popularity has been

Kennel Clubs

The American Kennel Club (AKC), founded in 1884, is the most influential dog club in the United States. The AKC is a "club of clubs," meaning that its members are other kennel clubs, not individual people. The AKC registers purebred dogs, supervises dog shows, and is concerned with all dog-related matters, including public education and legislation. It collects and publishes the official standards for all of its recognized breeds.

The United Kingdom version of the AKC is called the Kennel Club. However, the Kennel Club's members are individual persons. The membership of the Kennel Club is restricted to a maximum of 1,500 UK members in addition to 50 overseas members and a small number of honorary life members. The Kennel Club promotes responsible dog ownership and works on important issues like canine health and welfare.

The Shih Tzu is a gentle soul who is endlessly adaptable to the needs of his humans.

astronomical. In just 36 years since AKC recognition, more has happened to the breed than during its hundreds of years of previous history. The Shih Tzu is now one of the most popular breeds in the world, especially in England, Japan, and Canada.

Still, this little dog remains true to his ancient roots. He doesn't care if he's popular or obscure. He is a gentle soul who is endlessly adaptable to the needs of the humans he lives with. He is, above all else, a superb companion dog.

The American Shih Tzu Club

The American Shih Tzu Club is the official breed club in the United States. This club oversees the well-being of the breed. It holds the Shih Tzu national specialty show every year and has regional affiliates throughout the country. The American Shih Tzu Club also oversees Shih Tzu rescue efforts, keeps historic records, and provides information about Shih Tzu to novice pet owners and experienced exhibitors alike. For details on the breed, including rescue contacts, visit the American Shih Tzu Club website at www.shihtzu.org.

Chapter 2

CHARACTERISTICS of the Shih Tzu

The typical Shih Tzu can be described as a "love sponge." This breed is generally mellow and highly adaptable to many kinds of living situations. They get along well with family members and strangers and are usually great buddies with other dogs or other animals. The Shih Tzu is one of the few toy breeds that almost always does well with children.

Of course, every breed has its downsides. A Shih Tzu isn't the dog for you if you're looking for a jogging buddy. He's much more likely to kiss a stranger than warn you that one is approaching. His coat also takes considerable attention, and most owners turn to a professional groomer for help.

This chapter will help you decide if a Shih Tzu is the right dog for you and your home.

SHIH TZU APPEARANCE AND THE BREED STANDARDS

There's no doubt about it: Shih Tzu are very appealing dogs. With their luxurious coats and sweet expressions, they are very attractive. More importantly, they each have very individual personalities. They are an unusual mix of independence with gentle warmth, a sense of humor with a sense of self-importance.

The Shih Tzu Standard

Every breed has a standard—a blueprint that describes the height, weight, color, head, tail, and even the toes of the breed. At dogs shows, every dog is judged on how well he conforms to the standard. (That's why dog show competition is often called *conformation* competition.) Just as no human "perfect 10" exists, no dog perfectly meets the standard for any breed. Certainly, a Shih Tzu who doesn't even come close to being a show dog can still be a wonderful pet.

So, why should someone who just wants a pet pay attention to the standard? The standard describes, physically and temperamentally, what makes a Shih Tzu different from every other breed of dog on the planet. A

When raised and treated with respect, Shih Tzu are friendly dogs who get along well with everyone.

breeder who uses the standard as her guide will create Shih Tzu who retain the sturdy structure, the friendly temperament, and the glorious coat of a well-bred Shih Tzu.

One of the advantages of owning a purebred dog is that you can be pretty sure how your dog will grow up to look and act. The guidelines created by the standard give Shih Tzu their relative uniformity across the nation and even around the world. Even if you would never dream of owning a show dog, purchase your dog or puppy from a breeder who cares about breeding to the standard.

The following description of the Shih Tzu is based on an interpretation of the American Kennel Club's breed standard. It is very similar to the United Kingdom's Kennel Club standard. Interestingly, Shih Tzu are one of the few breeds to be classified in different groups in the two countries. They're shown in the Toy Group in the United States and in the Utility Group in England. (The Utility Group is basically equivalent to the U.S. Non-Sporting Group and includes such hard-to-classify breeds as Bulldogs, Dalmatians, and Bichon Frises.) To read both standards in their entirety, refer to the Appendix.

General Appearance

Both standards say that a Shih Tzu has an "arrogant carriage." The Kennel Club standard adds that the dog should have a chrysanthemum-like face. In either standard, this certainly sounds like a dog who would have been at home in the palaces of China centuries ago!

Size and Proportion

Shih Tzu are slightly longer than they are tall. They are compact little dogs, with good substance. A Shih Tzu's ideal height is 9 inches (23 cm) to 10½ (27 cm) inches at the withers (the top of the should blade). The ideal weight is 9 pounds (4.5 kg) to 16 pounds (7.5 kg) when mature.

Head

Shih Tzu are what dog show judges often call a "head breed"—the head and expression defines the appearance of the dog. A Shih Tzu has a round, broad head, short nose, and a warm, sweet, wide-eyed, friendly, and trusting expression that shows how gentle and loving a Shih Tzu is.

Body

This is a sturdy little dog who can enjoy long walks and have fun. Unlike some toy breeds, most Shih Tzu can move as efficiently as a larger breed.

Coat

The Shih Tzu coat is luxurious, double-coated, dense, long, and flowing. Shih Tzu aren't trimmed at all for the show ring other than to trim a bit around their paws for traction and neatness. The hair on the dog's head is always tied in a topknot (usually held in place with a brightly colored bow that may have sparkles on it).

Colors

The Shih Tzu is one of the few breeds of dogs for which all colors and combinations of colors are accepted. Enjoy the rainbow of possibilities with this breed!

Tail

The heavily plumed, high-set tail carried over the dog's back balances out the head and topknot. This is an entirely natural breed, and the ears and tail are never docked or cropped.

Shih Tzu at a Glance:

Size?
About 9 pounds (4.5 kg) to 16 pounds (7.5 kg).

Good apartment dogs?
Yes!

Good for traveling?
Yes!

Grooming needs?
High to very high.

Good with children?
One of the best small dogs with children. They shouldn't have to put up with toddlers or rambunctious behavior, but they are usually good family pets.

Good with other dogs?
Yes, but no roughhousing with large dogs.

Good with cats?
Yes.

Exercise needs?
Minimal to modest.

The breed standard attests that the Shih Tzu is inherently affectionate and outgoing.

Temperament

All American breed standards are required to mention breed temperament. The Shih Tzu standard goes far beyond what you'll find in most standards, however, and gives a beautiful description of the breed's personality. It says, "As the sole purpose of the Shih Tzu is that of a companion and house pet, it is essential that its temperament be outgoing, happy, affectionate, friendly, and trusting towards all." Remember, this standard determines how judges place dogs at a show. It's a rare standard to put so much emphasis on temperament—and it says a lot about this little breed.

IS A SHIH TZU RIGHT FOR YOU?

Shih Tzu are generally mellow dogs. They're highly adaptable and do well in condos, traveling in RVs, and living with single people or families. Still, that doesn't mean that every person should have a Shih Tzu. Here are some things to consider when you're deciding if a Shih Tzu fits your lifestyle.

Grooming Requirements

You may have fallen in love with that flowing, luxurious coat you see at dog shows. It takes hours of dedicated work every week to keep that kind of glorious coat. Don't even dream about it if you aren't willing to spend more time on your dog's hairdo than your own.

Most Shih Tzu are kept in either a puppy clip (a short version of the longer show coat) or cuts that are designed to look a bit like a Cocker Spaniel or Schnauzer. Even these comparatively easy "do's" take effort. Some Shih Tzu require daily brushing and combing. Even if you take your dog to a groomer, you will need to keep the dog combed daily between grooming visits.

If you use a professional groomer (which most pet owners do), it can also add up to a significant expense during the year. Do not consider a Shih Tzu for a pet if you want a simple, "wash and wear" kind of dog.

Because he is a heavily coated breed, your Shih Tzu requires regular grooming, even in a puppy clip.

Exercise Needs

Shih Tzu make great apartment dogs and can usually get enough exercise by chasing balls in the living room and following you around the house. While they appreciate and enjoy a leisurely stroll, these dogs certainly aren't exercise junkies. In fact, to keep them healthy and fit, some Shih Tzu must be encouraged to get more exercise than they might naturally choose.

Although this easygoing dog is ideal for some people, he's not what other people want. Are you a jogger? A Shih Tzu won't be your jogging buddy, unless you push him along with you in a doggy stroller. Do you love to throw a Frisbee at the beach for a Border Collie? Most Shih Tzu will just look at you when you are so foolish as to throw away your toy.

Consider at your lifestyle, and pick a dog who's right for you.

Watch Dog?

Although most toy breeds are barky, most Shih Tzu are quiet little dogs. They may not bark at someone who comes to your home. He's the kind of "watch dog" who watches while the bad guy steals your television and your jewelry.

The Shih Tzu makes a great choice for a condo dog, but doesn't provide the security of a more verbal dog if you live alone or worry about intruders.

Trainability

Shih Tzu are often labeled as stubborn. That's not really fair. Most Asian breeds have an independent streak, and Shih Tzu are no exception. The best way to train a Shih Tzu is to convince the dog it was his idea to do the task. (Food rewards can help that along!)

Understand your Shih Tzu, and you'll find him surprisingly easy to train. Shih Tzu are very smart and trainable, but it's important to use today's modern methods that make training a fun game. If you try to use coercion, you'll find yourself at constant odds with your little dog. No human has ever truly won a battle of the wills with a determined Shih Tzu.

(See Chapter 6 for obedience training that is designed to work positively with your little guy's independent spirit.)

They Aren't Like a Purse

Ever since a Chihuahua stole the show in the movie *Legally Blonde*, toy dogs have become a fashion statement. Starlets clutch their little dogs to their breasts everywhere they go.

Fashion statements come and go. Your dog isn't like a purse that you can change with the seasons. Remember, with luck, a Shih Tzu will live well into his teens.

Think before you get a Shih Tzu, no matter how appealing the dog may be. This is a 10- to 14-year commitment. Is this the right time in your life to make that commitment?

Just because small dogs are fashionable right now doesn't make a Shih Tzu the best dog for you. Think about what this great little breed needs from an owner, and decide if you're the person to provide that for a dog.

Companionability

Maybe it's because Shih Tzu have lived with humans for hundreds, if not thousands, of years, but this breed has perfected being a companion. They seem to sense the moods of their owners—and even of strangers.

Many people volunteer with Shih Tzu as animal-assisted therapy teams, visiting hospitals, nursing homes, special education classes, and other places where a warm puppy makes life seem better. With their almost human expression and delightful sense of humor, Shih Tzu can usually succeed in lightening any mood.

Shih Tzu and Children

Most toy dogs aren't a good combination with small children. If the children are past the toddler stage and are well behaved, most Shih Tzu are an exception to this rule. They are usually sturdy enough to enjoy playing with children and gentle enough not to be aggressive.

Taking the time to understand your Shih Tzu will assist you with his care and training.

Young Children

This doesn't mean that small children should be allowed to make the dog's life miserable. Every animal has his limits! It's not okay for children to pull on the dog's fur or poke around the dog's face with inquiring fingers. No dog should ever be left alone with a young child—for the sake of both, they need adult supervision.

A responsible Shih Tzu breeder will certainly want to meet your children before allowing a dog to come to your home.

Not All Shih Tzu Have Read the Books

Whenever you read about Shih Tzu, you will learn they are mellow little dogs who get along with everyone. As a general rule, that's true.

Of course, not every dog follows the general rule! Occasional Shih Tzu are much higher-energy dogs who like to run and romp and play. Although most Shih Tzu are peaceful and friendly with people, other dogs, and cats, a very small but noticeable minority are possessive of their toys and territory, and a rare few have been known to bite.

Each dog is an individual. Don't make assumptions about an individual until you know the dog.

Children and Shih Tzu get along famously when the children treat the dog properly.

This is a chance to be sure your children respect animals, and equally important, to be sure that this is a dog who will enjoy living with kids.

Older Children

Older children and Shih Tzu can be a winning combination. A special camaraderie develops between an older, responsible child and a lap-sized dog. Remember, though, kids are kids, and even the best child might not attend to details like an adult. Be especially careful to check the Shih Tzu's coat every day to be sure he's getting enough grooming. Don't let the dog suffer because an absent-minded adolescent became immersed in the school play, algebra homework, or discovered puberty and neglected to comb the dog's easily tangled coat.

Do not ever let a dog suffer because a child loses interest in caring for him! If you allow your child to have a pet, you must be willing to step in and care for the Shih Tzu if your child can't or won't do the job. Letting an animal suffer to teach the child a lesson only teaches your child that pets' feelings and physical comfort don't really matter. That's not what you want a child to learn.

Shih Tzu and Other Dogs

Shih Tzu generally get along well with other dogs. Unlike some breeds, no more aggression is apparent in either males or females, and Shih Tzu usually get along equally well with same-sex and opposite-sex dogs of all breeds.

Still, even dogs of friendly breeds need social experiences if they are to deal well with other dogs. The more experienced your puppy is in social interactions with other dogs, the less likely he is to get into trouble. Start by leaving him with his breeder until he's 12 weeks old, so he's learned to play appropriately with his littermates under his mom's watchful eye.

Seek out other small dogs for your Shih Tzu to play with. Check with other Shih Tzu owners in your community and invite a couple over for a play date. Other small breeds can make good friends for play dates with your little guy.

What Is an Imperial or Teacup Shih Tzu?

You may have seen ads for "Imperial" Shih Tzu or "Teacup" Shih Tzu. These are warning signs that you aren't dealing with a reputable breeder. These buzzwords are merely marketing terms for Shih Tzu who will supposedly be smaller than the typical Shih Tzu.

Read the breed standard, and you'll understand that these dogs were never intended to be tiny. Shih Tzu should be sturdy and hearty. In fact, their unparalleled abilities as therapy dogs and their good natures with children come in part because they aren't as breakable as most other toy dog breeds. Buying from someone who is changing those characteristics doesn't do this ancient dog any favors. The American Shih Tzu Club warns, "Those desiring a very tiny pet should choose another breed rather than destroying the very characteristics that make the Shih Tzu such an ideal companion."

Playing With Big Dogs

Under no circumstances should you let your Shih Tzu roughhouse with a dog who is substantially bigger than he is! Even though a Shih Tzu is relatively sturdy, he is only the size of a baby. He can get hurt if a friendly Labrador Retriever enthusiastically gives him a body slam. Don't take that risk.

It's great for your Shih Tzu to have full-sized friends. Let them go for walks together or hang out peaceably together, but no wrestling, no chase games, and no nipping. Not ever.

Well-socialized Shih Tzu can get along with other dogs.

Ask Your Dog to Behave When Near Other Dogs

Although most Shih Tzu are calm around other dogs, a few are aggressive. Too many small-dog owners think it's funny or even adorable when their little dogs bark or charge at big dogs. It's not. The big dog is likely to respond to your dog's aggression with his own aggression—and the big dog wins. It's not acceptable for a Rottweiler or a Doberman Pinscher to snarl, snap, and lunge at another dog, and it's not acceptable for your Shih Tzu, either.

(Later in this book, you'll learn about the Watch Me command, which teaches your dog to look at you, rather than getting tough with the big guys.)

Living With Big Dogs

If you already have a calm, gentle, larger dog at home, most likely that big guy and your Shih Tzu will become friends. Still, take precautions to prevent a disaster. Make clear rules and keep them. Don't let the dogs take each other's toys, and don't ever tolerate snapping or growling from either dog. A scene that would be a minor squabble between same-size siblings can become a calamity when one dog is small and the other dog is large.

Even if your Shih Tzu and your big bruiser are best buddies, don't leave them loose together when they are unsupervised. All it takes is a misplaced paw or an out-of-control skid while they're playing tag, and you'll come home to tragedy.

Shih Tzu and Other Creatures

Most Shih Tzu and cats get along famously. These gentle dogs even leave mice, rats, and birds alone—usually. However, under that adorable fur, a Shih Tzu is still a dog. You can never be sure that your child's pet mouse or bird won't awaken the hunter in your Shih Tzu. If a family member has rodents for pets, make sure that your Shih Tzu is never out with the animals unless an adult is there to supervise. Close off any rooms with prey animals when you leave your Shih Tzu at home alone.

In short, a Shih Tzu can be a delightful pet, as long as you are committed to spending the time and effort to care for him. These love-sponges fit in with a wide variety of families and living conditions, and they love to be with their human companions.

Comparing Lhasa Apsos and Shih Tzu

A lot of people get Lhasas and Shih Tzu confused. It's easy to see why: Both are similar in size and have long hair that falls to the floor, drop ears, and tails that curl over their backs. But take a look under all that hair, and you'll see some very significant differences between the two breeds.

Size: The size and proportions are similar, but the Shih Tzu can be smaller. The Shih Tzu is slightly longer than he is tall, whereas the Lhasa standard merely says that dogs of this breed are longer than they are tall.

Coat: Both have long, heavy coats that are parted down the middle of the dog's back. Both breed standards accept any coat color. In the show ring, a Shih Tzu always has a topknot, whereas a Lhasa's hair is parted on the top of his head and the "bangs" fall on both sides of the dog's nose.

Head: The biggest physical differences between the two breeds are the shape of their heads and the dogs' expressions. A Shih Tzu head is round and broad. The skull is domed. The muzzle is less than an inch long. A Lhasa Apso muzzle should be medium length. The dog's head should never be domed or wide, but instead be narrow and fall away behind the eyes.

Eyes: The dogs' eyes are very different. Shih Tzu eyes are large and round, placed well apart, and have a warm, sweet, wide-eyed, friendly, trusting expression. The Lhasa Apso standard is less descriptive, but says this breed should have eyes that are neither very large and full, nor very small and sunk.

Temperament: The biggest difference between the breeds is temperament. Although both breeds can be independent, Lhasas are "gay and assertive, but wary of strangers." Shih Tzu have no such suspicions. In fact, their standard says they should be "outgoing, happy, affectionate, friendly, and trusting toward all."

Shih Tzu and cats are known to get along together.

Chapter 3

PREPARING *for Your Shih Tzu*

You've made the big decision: A Shih Tzu is the right dog for your lifestyle. You know the upsides and downsides of the breed, and you're ready for a commitment of 10 to 14 years with a Shih Tzu. You've just taken the first step on your journey.

Each Shih Tzu has a unique personality, and you'll want to find the little dog who perfectly fits you. Remember, there aren't any "right" or "wrong" answers—but there are right and wrong answers for *you*.

But even picking the right dog isn't the whole story. We live in a big, noisy, strange world, and it's your job to help your new family member feel comfortable in it. Selecting the right Shih Tzu for you, preparing for him, and getting him off to a healthy start will make all the difference in the world. Take care now, and you'll have a lifetime of happy, bonded, loving times ahead. Don't do it right at the beginning, and you will regret it for years to come.

PRELIMINARY DECISIONS

When a child is born, the first question always asked is "Is it a girl or a boy?" Most people ask themselves the same question when they're planning to bring home a new dog. Then, of course, there's the other big question: puppy or adult?

Male Versus Female

In some breeds, the males and females have very different personalities. The Shih Tzu isn't one of them. These dogs have perfected being great companion dogs for millennia. Both males and females are usually easygoing, people-loving, animal-friendly souls.

Remember, when you're choosing your Shih Tzu, each dog is an individual with his own personality traits.

In this breed, don't worry about gender. Pick the puppy who captures your heart, and check the "plumbing" later. Since it's always best to neuter pet dogs (more on that later!), it really doesn't matter which gender steals your heart. In some breeds, it's important to purchase a dog of the opposite sex if you already have one dog, to prevent squabbles. Happily, most Shih Tzu get along equally well with their own gender or the opposite sex, so that's another issue you generally don't have to consider with this breed.

It's usually easier to find males for sale, especially if you are purchasing a dog from a show breeder. These breeders tend to part with females reluctantly, and only when the dog isn't the right choice for a breeding program.

Pet Versus Show Quality

It's a rare dog, even from the best breeders and the best bloodlines, who succeeds in the show ring. Some of the most fabulous pets are those dogs who almost, but didn't quite, make the grade as a show dog. Sometimes, even experienced show people have to minutely examine a "pet-quality" dog to see why the dog isn't winning in the show ring. The dog might have brown rather than black pigment around his eyes. His tail set may be a little too low, or his eyes might be just a smidgen too close together. A common fault is a male whose testicles didn't descend. However, your dog could be drop-dead gorgeous in all the parts the public will ever see and still be a pet-quality dog.

It is important to ask why the puppy or adult didn't make the grade as a show dog, however. For example, if you want a Shih Tzu who will do animal-assisted therapy, you don't want a dog who "washed out" of the ring because he was too shy. If you have dreams of agility competition or want a dog who loves to take long walks with you, then you don't want the dog who didn't make the grade because he didn't have sound knees or hips. A great breeder wants the perfect home for her dog just as much as you want to find the right dog for you. Working together, you'll find the match.

Remind yourself why you want a Shih Tzu so that you can realize your pup's potential as a show dog, performance dog, or companion.

Puppy Versus Adult

Ah, puppy breath. It's more seductive than new car smell. It's no wonder most people buy puppies. And little, round-faced, wide-eyed Shih Tzu puppies are certainly appealing. The plus of buying a puppy is that you have the chance to make sure he gets the ideal start in life. You can take him with you to meet people and sign him up for puppy kindergarten. It's fun to get your little guy off on the right paw.

There is equal joy in bringing home an adult dog. If you work outside the home, housetraining a Shih Tzu puppy can be a frustrating task. An adult comes already housetrained and doesn't need potty breaks every 20 minutes. And that doesn't count the odd things that puppies decide to destroy while they're teething. Puppyhood is definitely overrated. If you've never brought home an adult dog, the big worry is whether you could possibly bond with that grown-up creature. After all, isn't bonding what happens in the puppy years?

Although some breeds do have trouble transitioning from one home to another, Shih Tzu most emphatically do not. Older dogs are so grateful for their new homes; it can bring tears to your eyes. A puppy just can't match the depth of commitment an older dog will give you. Ask anyone who's brought home both adults and puppies over the years, and she will tell you

Puppy Buyer Checklist

- the puppy's registration form, or a signed agreement for a registration after the puppy has been neutered
- the puppy's pedigree
- your copy of the contract
- a list of the puppy's vaccines to date that you can give to your veterinarian
- your puppy's feeding instructions
- the breeder's phone number in case you have any questions or problems

that every dog fills up your whole heart. You will never feel a second-rate love for your secondhand dog.

Although many adults looking for homes are rescues, others are "change of career" dogs. He may be a retired champion who wants to be a family pet. She might be a retired mom who's had a couple litters of puppies and now wants someone to dote on her. He could even be a young adult who grew just a hair too tall for the show ring. All these dogs can make great pets.

Shih Tzu typically live 10 to 14 years. If you bring home an adult, you will likely have many satisfying, loving years together.

Is Two Better Than One?

Shih Tzu are such pleasant, social little dogs that many people come to a realization: They don't want just one. Two Shih Tzu are wonderful for keeping each other company if you're at work during the day. Almost all Shih Tzu love other dogs—especially other Shih Tzu. They will entertain and stimulate each other.

Unlike some breeds, Shih Tzu males and females all get along. You can have opposite-sex or same-sex "siblings" without expecting any aggression.

It's best to wait until you've had your first Shih Tzu for about a year before considering a second one. This gives you plenty of time to form a close bond with your first dog—and to know his personality well so that you can pick a good buddy for him.

How you treat the dogs' interactions during the first few days may determine whether the two dogs will become mortal enemies or best friends.

Here are some tips:

- **Let them meet on neutral territory.** Don't just waltz into the house with a new dog and expect him to be your first Shih Tzu's best friend. This can be upsetting to even a mild-mannered little guy. Ideally, let the dogs meet someplace neutral, such as an area at the breeder's home that is unfamiliar to both dogs or a get-acquainted room at the shelter. Sometimes, greetings outside your home aren't practical. At the very least, take both dogs on a walk together before bringing the new one into the house. This lets them meet on neutral turf, and the act of going on a walk together is often a bonding process.

Puppies are irresistible, but adult dogs have their advantages—and charms—as well, and make excellent companions.

- **Give more attention to the first dog for the first 2 weeks.** The best rule of thumb: Give the first dog 75 percent of the attention for the first 2 weeks. Instead of feeling left out, your dog will see the puppy as something that gives him even more attention than before. The puppy won't care, because 25 percent of your attention is more than he got when he had to share the limelight with his littermates and his mom. In about 10 days to 2 weeks, you'll see both dogs happy and relaxed; then you can begin giving both dogs equal attention.
- **Even after you're giving both dogs the same amount of attention,** don't forget to give the first dog a few extra perks. Greet him first when you come in the door. Feed him first. Always set aside special time alone with each dog—they both want some time just with you.

Shih Tzu almost always love other Shih Tzu. A second little dog can be a very happy addition to your household, if there's room in your schedule, pocketbook, and heart to care for two.

Responsible breeders can assure you that all their dogs are socialized and well cared for.

WHERE TO PURCHASE YOUR SHIH TZU

When you buy a Shih Tzu, how you spend your money affects the lives of other Shih Tzu. You must decide if you're going to support kind, honest people who care about the breed, or whether you're going to support people who will make a buck by skimping on the care of dogs. It's up to you.

Shih Tzu are one of the world's most popular breeds. Unfortunately, that means many of them are bred at puppy mills or by people who don't care about the welfare of the dogs and only want to make a profit.

Do you want to buy a puppy who has been raised in a cage? Do you want a dog from someone who sees every bit of that dog's puppyhood as a profit and loss statement? The more a breeder skimps on medical care, high-quality food, and even paying people to keep the place clean, the more she'll make.

Puppies who do not receive adequate human attention won't adjust to their new homes as well as puppies who have been handled and played with. Studies have shown that early and careful stimulation of young puppies improves their long-term health, ability to accept new situations and new people, attitude toward other dogs, and even their ability to learn and think. These puppies end up smarter than other dogs.

Puppies do best when they have nurturing mothers, a variety of experiences with new places, and plenty of interaction with humans.

Good breeders touch and hold their puppies from the day they are born. They make sure that the puppies walk on different surfaces, such as carpet, grass, and cement. Gentle children come over to play with the puppies. Puppies also learn how to react correctly to other dogs from their interaction with their littermates and their mom, so a responsible breeder doesn't let her Shih Tzu pups leave until they're at least 12 weeks old.

Compare that with a Shih Tzu pup born and raised in a cage. He's taken away from his mom at 6 weeks of age. He's never played in grass, never met a child, and never met anyone other than the kennel owner or her staff. He leaves home before experience with other dogs has taught him the rules of play, and he's likely to never get the hang of it.

Beware the Internet

Hundreds of thousands of dogs are sold over the Internet every year. Although perfectly good people can use the Internet as a wonderful way to communicate, it's also a major tool for puppy mills. Think about it: It bypasses all federal inspection and care requirements that have been established for the commercial pet industry. If you see ads for Shih Tzu on the Internet, proceed with extreme caution. It's easy for a puppy mill to present itself as a loving home in the suburbs.

Now, Where Do You Want to Buy Your Shih Tzu Puppy?

It sometimes takes patience. The best breeders aren't breeding to sell you a dog. The best ones are trying to breed dogs who reflect the breed standard and bring the breed forward in appearance, structure, and temperament. You may have to put your name on a waiting list to get a dog from this breeder. Is it worth it? You bet it is—both for you and for your future puppy.

Signs of a Responsible Breeder

Of course, no breeder is going to say, "I'm a puppy mill." Breeders will tell you their dogs are lovingly raised underfoot. A quick look will tell the truth. Here are some things to check for:

- **The odor is pleasant.** Take a deep breath in the area where the puppies live. If you're wrinkling your nose, leave. Cleanliness is one sign of a good breeder. Shih Tzu puppies should live inside the breeder's house, which should be a pleasant place to be.
- **Mom is a happy dog.** Pet the mother. Is she friendly? Is her coat clean? Does she smell good? If you feel sorry for her, you don't want to buy one of her puppies. If you do, you will only ensure that she is bred again.
- **The puppies have room to move around.** Of course, puppies have to be confined for their own safety, but this doesn't mean they have to be kept in small wire cages stacked on top of each other. It doesn't mean a cardboard box that reeks of urine. It can be something like a nice corner of the family room, with the puppies in an exercise pen or a whelping box. The puppies should be allowed supervised play in the house and, weather permitting, outside.
- **You shouldn't feel like you're "rescuing" the puppies.** If you buy from someone just to get a puppy away from a

If the mother dog seems healthy and well-adjusted, and the facilities are clean, signs are good that the breeder is raising her dogs right.

bad situation, think of what you're doing. You're financially rewarding the breeder for being evil to dogs. Of course, if the breeder makes money from you, she'll just put the mom through another pregnancy in 6 months. If you think you can't step away from a bad situation because you feel sorry for the puppy, walk away for the sake of the mom. A conscientious breeder will take responsibility for the lives of the puppies. She will take a 10-year-old dog back if the owner has to go to a nursing home. That's not the same as doing the minimum requirements.

- **A reputable breeder has only one or two breeds of dogs.** You can't be an expert in five or six breeds. A devoted breeder knows the history of her breed and the heritage of her dogs. She is successful in the show ring. She can't wait to show you the puppy's pedigree. She can show you generations of pedigrees and explain exactly why she bred one dog to another. She's also a member of the American Shih Tzu Club and subscribes to its code of ethics.

Signs of an Irresponsible Breeder

Warning signs are a tip-off that you're not working with an ethical breeder. Think twice, and think again, before buying a dog if:

The breeder you work with should want you to have a happy, healthy Shih Tzu for a lifetime; be wary of someone who just wants to make a sale.

- **The breeder advertises "Imperial" or "Teacup" Shih Tzu.** Shih Tzu should be sturdy little dogs when they are mature adults. Advertising "Imperial" or "Teacup" Shih Tzu is a marketing gimmick designed to snare naïve, unknowledgeable buyers. Don't be that buyer!
- **The puppy's parents are registered with a registry other than the American Kennel Club (AKC), the United Kennel Club (UKC), or the Kennel Club (KC).** In recent years, the AKC has enforced requirements for minimal health and record-keeping standards for high-volume breeders. Puppy mills created their own so-called registries that have none of the AKC's requirements. If you see registration for any organization other than the AKC, UKC or KC, don't consider a puppy from that breeder.
- **The dogs aren't registered at all.** Serious breeders who care about Shih Tzu register their breeding stock. Always.
- **The breeder suggests meeting in a park, a freeway rest stop, or your home—anyplace but hers.** She should be eager to show you the clean, healthy place where her puppies live. If she isn't, you have to wonder why.
- **The puppies are less than 12 weeks old.** Shih Tzu puppies, like other small breeds, take a little extra time to mature. The only reason to place puppies under 12 weeks of age is to get more of a profit sooner. Under no circumstances should you ever consider bringing home a puppy younger than 10 weeks old.
- **There are dogs you don't get to see.** A great breeder is

Because Shih Tzu are so popular, you may have to wait for the puppy best suited for you.

proud of her dogs. She can't wait for people to meet them. If she's hiding them away from view, ask yourself why.

- **The breeder has too many dogs.** By definition, breeders have more dogs than most of us. If a breeder is showing dogs and has a litter of puppies every year or so, she probably has more Shih Tzu at her house than you do at yours. Still, there is a limit to how many dogs a person can care for successfully. A good hobby breeder may have more dogs than most people, but she will never have 50. If you see Shih Tzu who need grooming and who don't seem to be comfortable with people—and if the house doesn't smell clean—you can assume the puppies in the litter you're looking at aren't getting the time and attention they should be.
- **The breeder doesn't ask you probing, personal questions about your life.** If she really cares about her puppies, the breeder wants to know what life is like at your house. Do you have a big dog in the house? How about a toddler? A fenced yard? What happened to other pets you've owned? They didn't end up at a shelter, did they? If she doesn't ask these kinds of questions, she doesn't care about the future of her puppies.
- **The place leaves you feeling uncomfortable.** Trust your instincts on this one. You don't owe a stranger an explanation for why you're not going to buy her puppy. If you get a bad feeling about the place and the puppies, walk away.

With the demand right now for toy dogs, it's easy to get frustrated. Some breeders have long waiting lists for their Shih Tzu. It's better to be patient and wait for a happy, socialized little puppy who has been loved since before he was born than to reward a greedy breeder with your money. You will be so glad you waited when the right dog from the right breeder comes along!

A breeder's puppies should appear happy and healthy.

Finding a Great Breeder

Now that you're committed to finding an ethical, caring breeder, there's just the problem of finding one. It's not like there's a section in the phone book that says "Ethical Shih Tzu Breeders." This section will tell you how to find one.

The American Shih Tzu Club is the breed club officially recognized by the AKC. It has a breeder referral committee that can recommend buyers to club members who have agreed to a code of ethics. The site also links to local affiliate Shih Tzu clubs around the country that can also give referrals for breeders who have agreed to the American Shih Tzu Club's ethics rules.

Of course, you should always check out the breeder personally, but a Shih Tzu club member is an excellent starting point.

Meeting Breeders at Dog Shows

Because the best breeders show their dogs, it only makes sense to go to a dog show when you're looking for a great breeder. Talk with people showing their dogs (when they're not busy), and get a sense of the dogs and the people who impress you. Every show has a catalog for sale that includes the name and mailing address for every exhibitor; this is a great resource for contacting prospective breeders. Make an appointment to meet with the breeders you like best. Even if they don't have puppies for sale, you will learn about the breed—and they might be able to refer you to a breeder with plans for an upcoming litter. Members of the local kennel club will staff the information desk at the dog show, and it's worth asking them if local club members have Shih Tzu puppies available. People active in their local clubs are usually ethical, caring breeders.

While you are at the show, stop and watch the obedience and agility trials that often accompany all-breed shows. If a Shih Tzu is entered, ask the owner where she got her dog. These competitors usually select their dogs based on temperament and physical soundness—traits you're looking for, too.

You may meet the breeder of your future puppy through the Internet, but you should still meet in person, if possible.

Finding Breeders Through Internet Lists

The Internet is full of specialized e-mail lists and chat groups for Shih Tzu lovers. These can be a good place to learn more about the breed and to form e-mail relationships with breed fanciers. Although most lists prohibit advertising, breeders often put a website address next to their names, which allows you to look at their dogs.

Just because someone sounds good when she's chatting on the Internet doesn't mean she's a conscientious breeder. Check out any breeder you meet on the Internet with the same healthy skepticism you would apply to any other Internet meeting.

Visiting the breeder will give you firsthand insight into how her puppies are raised and treated.

Finding Breeders Through Newspaper Ads

Most reputable breeders are averse to advertising in newspapers, but some do advertise. Look at people who advertise Shih Tzu in the paper with the same caution you'd look at people who advertise cars in the paper. Check them out thoroughly—don't just rely on how they describe themselves.

The Breeder and Buyer Interviews

Visiting the breeder gives you a chance to see if she's the person from whom you want to buy a dog, and it gives the breeder a chance to see if you're the right person for one of her puppies. It's a mutual interviewing process.

Expect the breeder to ask prying, probing, personal questions. She'll ask questions like:

- Do you have children or expect to have children? Do you

have grandchildren who visit frequently? Most Shih Tzu are good with children, but some prefer an adult-only home.

- How will you pay for veterinary emergencies? You don't need to be wealthy, but the breeder needs to know you're committed to caring for the dog.
- Do you work outside the home? Do you travel on business? If so, what arrangements will you make for your dog when you're not there?
- What is your home like? It makes a difference if you live in a condo (where you need a dog who doesn't bark) or the country. If you have a home full of rare antiques, you may need a mellow dog who is past his chewing phase.
- How active are you? If you like to hike, you'll probably want a different kind of dog than will someone who just wants to share the couch with a dog.

Although picking the right puppy should be done with your head and your heart, it often feels like something that just "happens" when you meet.

- The breeder may even insist on a home visit. Welcome it. She wants her dogs to find the perfect "forever" home. A great breeder knows her dogs' souls; the more she knows about you, the better chance she has of helping you find the Shih Tzu who will be your soul mate.

You need to ask her questions, too:

- Why did she decide to breed the parent dogs of the puppies?
- How long have the dogs on the puppy's pedigree lived? (You want a puppy who has a lot of relatives who lived into their teens.)
- What health screenings have the parents had?
- How does she socialize her puppies?
- Is she active in Shih Tzu clubs or local kennel clubs?

Think about the breeder's communication style. You want someone who can help you if you have questions and problems with your puppy. It doesn't matter whether you agree with the breeders' personal politics, admire her décor, or want to be her best friend (although you might find your best friend—you never know). What *does* matter is that you respect the way she treats her dogs and that you can communicate well with her, so if you do get a puppy, you can utilize her wisdom.

Let the Magic Happen

You've picked a puppy from a great source. You've been patient—maybe you've even seen several litters before you've found the litter that impresses you.

Now, it's time to enjoy the magic connection that happens when you and your puppy choose each other. You'll look at the puppy, he'll look at you, and you'll know he's the right one. You'll look into his eyes and think, "That's my dog!" And that little Shih Tzu puppy will be looking at you, undoubtedly thinking, "That's my human!"

RESCUE ME!

There is a great alternative to purchasing a puppy. Instead, consider adopting a Shih Tzu who needs a home.

Shih Tzu are one of the most popular breeds in the United States and in much of the world. Sadly, that means a lot of dogs need homes. Some are dogs whom people bought on a whim when they walked past a pet store—and quickly developed buyer's remorse. Others were beloved family pets whose homes could no longer keep them. Sometimes puppy mills dump their dogs after they aren't useful for breeding anymore.

Although few puppies are found in rescue, a lot of wonderful adult dogs are just waiting for someone to love them. Some may have special needs, such as medical problems or behavior issues. Others are shy and need an understanding owner who will devote the time and patience to help them build confidence. Still others are outgoing, absolutely healthy little dogs who can't wait to share their joy with a forever home.

Indefinite Listing Privilege

Until several years ago, unregistered dogs couldn't compete in AKC events. Now they can! The AKC has an Indefinite Listing Privilege for altered purebred dogs. You can download the form at the AKC website (www.akc.org). Dogs with ILP numbers can compete in dog sports, including agility, obedience, and rally obedience. Go have fun with your second-chance dog!

Responsible rescue groups will be just as prying as a responsible breeder. They've seen the toll it takes on a dog to be abandoned, and they don't want it to happen to these little guys again. Expect the group to check out your home extensively and ask for references from your veterinarian.

Expect a lot of honesty from rescue groups. They want you to know the dog's quirks before you commit to the animal. You'll know about any problems, such as a dislike of cats or kids, or any existing health issues. Of course, some Shih Tzu come to rescue groups with no known history; the rescue organization can only tell you what it knows.

Responsible rescue groups will *always* require you to alter your dog. Many are now altering Shih Tzu before they go to their new homes.

Finding a Rescue Shih Tzu

The American Shih Tzu Club has members who are devoted to helping any Shih Tzu find a safe and loving home.

Petfinder.com is one of the most wonderful sites on the Internet. It links rescue groups and shelters from around the country with people who want to adopt a "secondhand" dog. You can see photos and descriptions of Shih Tzu from all over the country who are looking for good homes.

To look at available dogs, just go to www.petfinder.com, select "Shih Tzu" from among the breeds, and enter your zip code. Instantly, Shih Tzu (and Shih Tzu mixes) looking for homes from rescue groups and shelters around the United States will come up on your screen. These listings are complete with photos, histories, and special needs (if any). The listings closest to your home will pop up first. On the day this chapter was written, more than 400 Shih Tzu and Shih Tzu mixes were listed on Petfinder.com. It's a great way to find a pet!

Shih Tzu also come to local shelters with surprising frequency. A small, adorable Shih Tzu is likely to quickly find a home, so get to know the shelter staff and volunteers so they'll know you're looking for a "secondhand" Shih Tzu. Many shelters keep "wish lists" for people looking for specific breeds.

PICKING THE RIGHT PUPPY FOR YOU

Picking a puppy must be done with both your head and your

Whatever the source of your Shih Tzu, he will thrive if you give him the care, attention, and training he needs.

heart. If you find a breeder you respect, ask for her guidance in picking the right puppy for you. She knows her dogs and will be able to predict which adorable ball of fuzz will grow up to be the dog you're looking for.

Shih Tzu, like other small dogs, tend to have small litters. It's not unusual for a mom to have only two or three puppies. This means that you don't have the luxury of comparing a lot of puppies with each other. It helps to have some specific criteria to think about when you're deciding if a puppy is right for you.

Here are some things for you to consider as you look at each puppy, no matter the source:

Appearance

Look for a puppy with bright eyes, a thick, fluffy coat, and good energy level. Also look for obvious physical problems, such as bowed legs or knees or hocks that aren't structured correctly.

Temperament

Even from a young age, Shih Tzu puppies have very distinct personalities. Some like action and are independent, while others are quiet and dependent. Think about the role you want your future dog to play in your life, and choose a puppy who matches those expectations.

Remember, puppies act differently when they're with their mom and littermates than they do when they're alone. Take each puppy into a room where he doesn't usually spend a lot of time. Talk with him. Play with him.

Keep in mind the adult dog you dreamed about when you decided you wanted a Shih Tzu. Did you want a cuddling dog who wants nothing more than to snuggle with you for hours on end? Then pick the puppy who settles into your arms like it's

Pups who have been exposed to myriad experiences and circumstances tend to be more secure and better socialized.

the place he was born to be. Do you like a more independent, active little buddy? Then select the one who looks for action and plays with toys.

One short visit won't tell you the whole story of a puppy's personality. For example, a puppy who seems too low-energy for you might just be ready for a nap. Ideally, visit the litter at least twice. A good breeder observes her puppies from the time they are born and can help you get a feel for their overall personalities.

Don't pick the pup who doesn't want to make eye contact with you or avoids you. This puppy might be shy, sick, or in pain. In any event, the dog isn't bonding with you.

Socialization

About half of a dog's makeup is genetically determined, and half comes from his experiences in life. Socialization during the first weeks of your puppy's life helps to determine the kind of dog he'll grow up to be. Some breeders say their puppies are well socialized (and might even believe it), but the puppies have never left the breeder's kitchen, never met a strange dog, and never met a child.

Shih Tzu should go to their new homes when they are 12 weeks of age or older. By that time, the breeder should ensure that:

- The puppies have been handled by people of all ages, especially children.
- They've walked and played on a variety of surfaces, including slippery flooring (such as linoleum) and carpet.
- They've played outside (weather permitting) in a safe area.
- They've ridden in a car.

Be sure to get all the necessary paperwork from your breeder and register your puppy in the time required.

IMPORTANT DOCUMENTS

Whether you've decided on a potential show dog or a dog who is just going to be best in show in your heart, you've done it! You have your soul mate wrapped in fur!

You must discuss a few important details with the source of your puppy, though, before you can live happily ever after with your dog.

Health Records

Puppies are given a series of vaccinations from about age 6 weeks to 4 months. Be sure to get a list of vaccinations that your puppy has received, so your veterinarian can be sure she isn't overvaccinating or undervaccinating your new dog when you bring him home.

Registration Papers

Ethical breeders never, ever breed a dog who isn't registered. Your puppy's parents should both be registered with the AKC or another reputable registry. The litter or individual puppies should also be registered.

Four registration options are available to a breeder—this list shows how they affect you:

1. *She may give you a registration application form for the puppy.*

Registering Your Shih Tzu in England

The English equivalent to the AKC is the Kennel Club (KC). Registration procedures in both countries are almost identical. Both of your puppy's parents must be registered, and the breeder must register the litter. The breeder will give you a registration certificate to fill out, and the Kennel Club will process the puppy's change of ownership.

For more information, check out the Kennel Club's website at www.the-kennel-club.org.uk.

If she does this, ask her if she wants you to use her kennel name when determining the registered name of your puppy. You then send in the registration application to the AKC to register your puppy.

2. *She may give you the puppy's registration application form upon proof of neutering.* Many responsible breeders will have a neuter contract for their puppies. You can get the registration application form after you show proof from your veterinarian that the puppy has been neutered.
3. *She may give you limited registration.* This new option is increasingly common. A limited registration is proof that you have a purebred dog and allows you to compete in obedience, agility, and other performance sports. (You will not be allowed to compete in conformation.) This registration only applies to your dog; it does not allow any puppies produced by your dog to be registered.
4. *She may register the dog herself.* Many breeders register their own puppies when they are young. They like to name their own dogs. This breeder will give you a fully registered dog.

Pedigree

A reputable breeder will give you a copy of your puppy's pedigree, which traces the puppy's family tree back three, four, or five generations.

A good check for the quality of the dog is to see how many champions show up on the pedigree. It's easy to find them, because champions' names are traditionally written in red. Serious breeders use mostly champions in their breeding programs, because these are dogs whom judges have determined meet the breed standard.

It's fun to read a pedigree with all the long-winded registered names of purebred dogs. But if you are buying from an excellent breeder, the pedigree means a lot more than just a list of your dog's ancestors' names. Your breeder should be familiar with the dogs on the pedigree and know how each one helps to contribute to the health, beauty, and character of the breed. You might not care much about the specifics, but you want to buy from the kind of breeder who is eager and proud to give you a copy of your dog's famous family tree.

Contract

If you're buying your dog from a reputable breeder, most likely you will be asked to sign a contract. This is written to protect your puppy. It may require you to neuter your puppy or return the puppy to the breeder if you decide not to keep the dog. It will also include the breeder's health guarantees. Like any other legal document, read it carefully and understand what you are signing.

Feeding Instructions

It's a big adjustment for a dog to leave his old home and come to yours. It will help him a lot if you keep him on the same diet and feeding schedule he's accustomed to for at least the first couple weeks. Your breeder should give you a feeding schedule. (If your dog is less than 6 months old, he's probably eating three times a day.) She should also tell you the kind of food and the amount; she may send a couple days' worth of food home with you when you pick up the puppy.

PREPARING YOUR HOME FOR THE NEW ARRIVAL

Before you bring your Shih Tzu home, you get to go shopping! Here's what your dog needs to get started:

Baby Gates and Ex Pens

Crates are great, but they aren't the whole answer to keeping your Shih Tzu safe. If you're gone for more than a few hours at a time, a crate won't allow your dog to move around or get a change of scenery. Sometimes, you'll want your dog to be with you but not underfoot. For example, if you're working on a craft project with items strewn around the house, you might want your little guy to be company for you, but you don't want him in the middle of the glitter that's been dipped in glue! For times like these, consider exercise pens or baby gates.

Exercise pens are convenient—they fold up for easy storage.

Baby gates provide a barrier

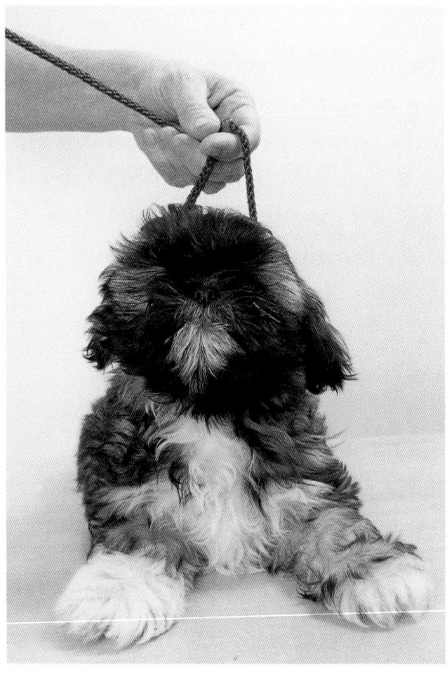

Your puppy will need a collar and leash. Select a style that's durable and comfortable for both of you to use.

between rooms. You can leave your little guy in the kitchen or bathroom, for example. He can see what's going on in other rooms, but he doesn't have the ability to leave the puppy-proofed bath or kitchen area. This gives your Shih Tzu some freedom but also keeps him away from the dangers found when roaming the house at will. You can find baby gates at pet supply stores, but check out prices in the baby departments of discount stores, where they are usually less expensive.

Exercise pens are folding, portable, wire or plastic fences that can be placed anywhere in your home. They're very convenient, because you can move them from room to room, and they fold up for easy storage when you're not using them.

Whether you are keeping your Shih Tzu in an exercise pen or in a safe room behind a door gate, always leave him in a confined area when you aren't home to supervise. He'll never get the hang of housetraining if you give him free range of the house while you're gone. He could also be needlessly exposed to household hazards, from curtain cords (that playful dogs have hanged themselves on) to exposed electric cords. Confining your puppy is important to ensure that he has a long and happy life.

Collar or Harness

Your puppy will need a collar or harness that fits him. Happily, small collars are getting easier to find as toy breeds become more popular. Major pet supply companies, catalogs, and online pet supply stores have a growing number of small-dog collars.

Adjustable collars with plastic snaps are great for growing

puppies. A small buckle collar will also work well. Remember, your puppy will grow quite a bit from the time he's a puppy until he reaches his full size. Be sure to check his collar regularly to make sure that it isn't getting too tight.

Don't buy a choke collar or a prong collar for your Shih Tzu. You don't need to give your little dog painful corrections to get him to mind you.

Many people with Shih Tzu prefer harnesses to collars, because harnesses don't put any pressure on the dog's throat. Look for a well-fitted, comfortable little harness.

Combing Under the Collar

Remember to comb the hair underneath your dog's collar or harness every day. This will help prevent matting and hair loss and will keep his skin healthier.

Crate

You need to see a crate the same way your Shih Tzu does. When you see a wire or plastic box, you probably think of a doggy prison. Your Shih Tzu sees the crate and thinks of a comfy den.

Your dog needs a quiet spot to rest when life is too noisy or busy in the rest of the house, and he needs a safe haven when you travel. A crate gives these things to your dog.

Here's how to make sure your Shih Tzu enjoys his crate:

- **Buy the right crate.** It must be large enough for your dog to stand, turn around, and lie down in.
- **Show your dog how to use his crate.** Begin by putting treats in the crate and telling your dog "go kennel." He'll learn that he gets a treat if he walks into his crate. After he's learned it's fun to enter his crate, briefly close the door. Over the course of a few days, gradually teach the dog to spend more time in his crate.
- **Use treats.** Treat-holding toys stuffed with peanut butter, kibble, or cheese are great pacifiers for dogs who take a while to adjust to a crate. Put the food-stuffed toy in the crate with your dog, and he'll spend time enjoying his yummy toy instead of complaining.
- **Place the crate in a central location.** Your dog is part of your family, and his crate should be in a place where the family gathers, such as the living room or den. (Dogs who sleep in their crates should have a crate in the bedroom, so nighttime isn't a lonely time.)
- **Feed your dog his meals in his crate.** He'll learn that the crate represents all that is good in the world.

Select size-appropriate chew toys for your puppy.

- **Never use the crate for punishment.** Don't put your dog in his crate because you are angry or because he's been "bad."
- **Be matter-of-fact when your dog goes in and out of the crate.** You aren't putting him in prison, and you aren't rescuing him from jail. He's just going in and out of his bedroom.

Food and Water Bowls

Make sure the food and water bowls are small enough for your short-nosed Shih Tzu to use comfortably. Replace the water in the bowl with clean water every day.

Identification

No matter how careful you are, your Shih Tzu can get lost. His best ticket home is identification. In fact, if you have both a tag and a microchip on your dog, chances are good that you'll get your dog back if he gets lost.

Tags

Your dog should always wear his collar and a tag with your name and phone number on it.

Microchip

A microchip is a rice-sized electronic chip your veterinarian injects under your dog's skin. Each microchip has a unique number. If your lost dog is brought to a shelter or veterinarian's office that has a scanner, the staff will be able to obtain the number. They then call the chip manufacturer to get your phone number. (Be sure to keep your contact information up to date with the chip manufacturer.)

Small, curious puppies can easily get into trouble if your home isn't puppy-proofed.

Leash

Find a nice lightweight leash. Nothing looks sadder than a little dog walking with a big, heavy leash. Chain leashes are too heavy, and they're hard on your hands. Always select a leather or fabric leash.

Toys

Most Shih Tzu thoroughly enjoy their toys and remain fond of them throughout their lifetimes. Toys are especially important for puppies, because they help with the teething process. Be sure your pup has toys that allow him to bite down and chew.

No formula exists for the perfect Shih Tzu toy, since each Shih Tzu has his favorites. Some love plush toys twice their size, while others enjoy chasing balls. Some prefer plastic squeaky toys. Take your dog with you to the pet supply store and ask him which ones he likes best. He'll tell you!

Whether your dog is a gentle player or one who loves to chew and shred, be very careful with any toys that have eyes, threads, or other pieces that can come loose and get stuck in his throat or digestive system. If your dog tears a toy apart, throw away any stuffing or squeakers. Swallowing one of these objects can be a medical emergency.

PUPPY-PROOFING YOUR HOME

Shih Tzu seem so levelheaded that you might be lulled into a false sense of security.

A puppy is a puppy. You never know what he will decide to climb over, bite into, or squirm through. Be sure your house is puppy-proofed before you bring your little guy home.

Don't Have These at Home

Two of the most dangerous products to your Shih Tzu are slug bait and traditional, sweet-tasting antifreeze. Don't have these in your home.

Slug bait causes the deaths of many dogs every year. It smells and tastes good to dogs but causes an agonizing death. Use nontoxic solutions to kill slugs. A few slugs in your yard are better than exposing your little guy to this lethal concoction.

Just 1 teaspoon (5 ml) of antifreeze can kill an adult Shih Tzu. Dogs like the sweet taste, and many die every year after lapping it up. Happily, new brands of antifreeze have a bitter taste and use less lethal ingredients. Use these brands instead.

- **Electrical cords.** A single bite on an electrical cord can kill your puppy. Cover all electrical cords; cord covers are available at computer stores and at many variety stores.
- **Household chemicals.** Cleaners, disinfectants, insecticides, and other chemicals should be stored in a high cabinet, where a curious puppy will never find them. Better yet, go green and try to use only nontoxic, earth-friendly (and Shih Tzu-friendly!) products.
- **Use pet-repellent sprays.** These harmless sprays have a very unpleasant taste or smell. Spray anything you don't want the dog to chew. Still, keep a careful eye on your puppy, because some dogs are unaffected by the sprays. You can find pet repellent sprays at pet supply stores.
- **Use door gates.** Put a door gate at the top of the stairs or to keep your puppy out of any room (such as a sewing room) that might contain sharp or dangerous objects.
- **Clear off low tables.** People with Great Danes must worry about what's on their kitchen counters, but people with Shih Tzu must be sure coffee tables and other low-lying areas are free of candy, precious family heirlooms, or photographs they don't want a curious puppy to chew.

THE HOMECOMING

You're ready for the big day—your new Shih Tzu is coming home! The next few days will be the time to make sure that your new puppy or adult dog bonds with you and feels at home.

Plan to take a week off. The time you spend with your dog now will pay off for years to come. Besides, who wants to be at work when you're thinking about your new dog at home?

Bringing Your Shih Tzu Home

Have a crate in the car when you pick up your dog. A crate will provide the safest ride home for him.

It's not unusual for puppies to get carsick, so be prepared. The crate should be lined with towels, so it's comfortable but you can easily clean things up if he gets carsick. Bring a couple of extra towels with you in case you need them.

If your drive is longer than a half hour or so, plan to make potty stops along the way. Be careful where you stop, especially if your new dog is a puppy who hasn't completed his

A comfy bed is a must, at home or on the road!

vaccination schedule. Avoid places where many dogs potty, such as rest stops, because this may be a place that could expose him to deadly parvo, distemper, or canine influenza viruses.

The First Two Days

The first couple of days should be a quiet time to get acquainted with your new dog. Many Shih Tzu are methodical little dogs who want to explore things at their own pace. Don't invite friends over until the dog has had a few days to get to know the cast of characters in the household first.

Some Shih Tzu will be wagging their tails with glee within minutes of coming home, but others are more cautious and will adjust more slowly. Don't force yourself on the dog, but do offer him fun games. Lie still and let him explore you. Let him fall asleep on your lap.

Sleeping Arrangements

Shih Tzu are happiest when they sleep in the same room as their families. Plan to let him sleep in your room.

Most Shih Tzu undoubtedly sleep with their owners. After all, most of these dogs are world-class snugglers. Most dogs and owners are perfectly fine sharing a bed. It's not like the little guys take up a lot of room. However, if you have a Shih Tzu who growls at you or your mate, he doesn't belong in your bed. Bedtime shouldn't be about who's in charge.

If you don't want your dog in your bed, or if he's growling or otherwise making the bed uncomfortable or unpleasant for you or your mate, give him a comfy crate in the bedroom. Because dogs are pack animals, they are happiest if they get to spend their sleeping time near their human "pack."

TRAVELING WITH YOUR SHIH TZU

Shih Tzu make great traveling companions. They're quiet. They're usually very calm. They just love to be with you. Use a few precautions and plan ahead so that you and your dog can have years of fun exploring new places together.

In the Car

If you decide to vacation without your Shih Tzu, consider hiring a pet sitter to care for him in your home.

Airbags can kill a small child, and they can certainly kill a Shih Tzu. You're exposing your dog to a terrible risk if you hold him on your lap or let him sit in the front seat when you drive. If you have front-seat airbags, be sure your dog *always* travels in the back seat!

Keep your little guy in a crate in the back seat. Be sure the crate is securely belted in and has comfy bedding for your dog. Consider it the same as a child's safety seat. Your dog will happily adjust to riding in his crate—he'll think this is how all dogs travel. And both of you will reach your destination safely.

In the Air

Almost all Shih Tzu are small enough to fly with you in the cabin on most major airline flights.

Check out the airline's rules before you decide to fly. Here are some things to think about when planning your trip:

• **Dogs must be in approved carriers especially designed to tuck underneath the seat.** Several companies make soft-sided, airline-

A dog walker can feed and exercise your Shih Tzu while you're at work.

approved carry-on bags for small dogs. Whatever brand you choose, they all look very much like conventional carry-on luggage, except for the netting that gives your pet ventilation. Because Shih Tzu are usually so quiet, other passengers probably won't even notice you're carrying a dog on board. These pet carriers are widely available at pet supply stores or online. Be sure the particular bag you select meets the airline's requirements.

- **Teach your Shih Tzu to enjoy his carrier.** If you've crate-trained your dog, you're well on your way to having a happy Shih Tzu traveler. Just teach him to enjoy the new carrier in the same way you taught him to enjoy his crate. Because you will be carrying this carrier with your dog in it, practice walking with him in the carrier. Most dogs adjust very well to airline travel.
- **Expect to pay additional fees, and make early reservations.** Airlines charge additional fees for pets in the cabin. Also, most airlines allow only one or two animals on each flight, so book your pet's travel arrangements well ahead of time.
- **Check the airline's website for their rules.**

Enjoy! Many small dog cross the country—and even the oceans—every day. Shih Tzu are among the best jet-setters in dogdom.

WHEN YOUR SHIH TZU CAN'T JOIN YOU

The odds are that you'll need to take some trips without your dog. Whether it's a business trip or a family funeral, there are places where even the most wonderful dogs don't belong. Plan ahead for those times when you may have to leave your Shih Tzu behind.

Bringing a Shih Tzu home is like adding a family member

Boarding Your Shih Tzu

Many dogs go to boarding facilities when their owners are out of town. Some great boarding facilities are like second homes to dogs. Others aren't so good. Check boarding facilities out long before you find you have to leave town the next day on an emergency.

Ask for recommendations of good local facilities. Your breeder, veterinarian, or groomer may be able to give you some great suggestions. No matter who recommends the facility, go for a personal visit. To really see what happens at the facility, go unannounced during regular business hours. Do you like what you smell? It should be extremely clean, even if it's an older facility. If a lingering odor is present, something is wrong. Do you like the feel of the place? Some boarding facilities are just more cheerful than others. Do the animals seem happy? Although some dogs adjust better than others to being left behind, none of the dogs should seem frightened. Most should seem cheerful. If the dogs aren't generally happy and relaxed, don't consider leaving your pet there.

Be clear about what services are offered. Do they give individual attention to each dog every day? Do they groom the dogs? Do the dogs go on walks? Do they have playtime with compatible dogs? Where will your dog sleep, and does it look comfortable for your Shih Tzu?

Some facilities charge extra for giving medication, feeding a particular dog food, grooming, and for supervised playtime. Others include these services as part of the basic price. Be sure to understand exactly what services are covered in the price, and what a day at the boarding facility will be like for your dog.

Be sure that the boarding kennel asks *you* questions. They should want to know things such as your dog's favorite activities, what cheers him up, and what you want to do in case of a medical emergency. If they don't ask these questions, how can they know the answers?

Make reservations ahead of time. The best places are sometimes booked a year ahead of time, especially for holidays.

Pet Sitters

Because they're quiet and generally well behaved, Shih Tzu are often a favorite with people who have jobs. Even the most perfect little dog might need some attention if you work long hours. It's not fair for your dog to live in a crate 8 or 12 hours a day with no stimulation, no potty breaks, and no human contact. Even patient little Shih Tzu have their limits.

Shih Tzu are usually little homebodies, and a pet sitter can be a better option than a boarding facility. These professionals come to your home two or more times a day. If you are going to be gone more than a day or so, you'll probably want to find one who will spend the night with your dog. (Although some pet sitters only visit during the day, others will stay at your home. For longer absences, it's a good idea to hire someone who will "live in.")

A pet sitter can come once or twice a day to entertain your Shih Tzu for about a half hour. Pet sitting services vary, but they may include a potty break, playtime, a walk, or even a playdate with a pre-approved, compatible small dog.

Most of the people in this business are truly wonderful, but you are giving the keys to your house and the responsibility for your four-legged family member to someone. Of course, you'll want to check references extremely carefully. Find a pet sitter near you by asking for recommendations from your veterinarian and groomer.

Doggy Day Care

In some communities, practically as many doggy day care facilities exist as there are coffee shops. This can be a great option for your Shih Tzu if he is a social little guy. It isn't a happy place for a dog who doesn't enjoy the company of other dogs.

Before you enroll your dog, spend time at the day care. Not all of them are safe places for small dogs. Be sure they separate big, rambunctious dogs from small or shy ones. A big dog should never be allowed to jump on a little one.

As long as the day care is set up with the needs of small dogs in mind, it can be a great place to let your little dog enjoy the company of other dogs. If it's done right, he'll have a great time playing while you're at work.

It can seem like a tall order to take so many steps to bring home just one little dog. Remember, though, that bringing a Shih Tzu home is adding a family member. You want to do it right. All the effort of finding the right dog and giving him the right start in life will pay off countless times in your many years of life together.

Chapter 4

FEEDING
Your Shih Tzu

What you feed your Shih Tzu—and how much—will make a big difference in the length of his life and how he feels every day.

Shih Tzu don't need to eat a lot to maintain their correct weight. This means it's important that every little mouthful your dog eats is packed with nutrition to keep him healthy and long lived.

Dog food should be easy, right? Just pour out it out of a bag or spoon it out of a can and you're good to go. Well, not anymore. In today's nutrition-conscious world, dozens of alternatives are available. A lot of contradictory advice is given about dog food, and this can overwhelm you. This chapter will help you sort out the alternatives and make choices that are right for you and your dog.

WHEN TO FEED

Puppies eat four meals a day from the time they're weaned from their mother's milk until they're 3 months old. Since reputable breeders don't sell Shih Tzu until they are at least 12 weeks old, those four-times-a-day feedings will be the breeder's job.

From ages 3 to 6 months, your puppy should get three meals a day. After he's 6 months old, you'll want to feed him twice a day.

Be sure to feed your Shih Tzu his last meal at least 3 hours before he goes to bed, to avoid nighttime housetraining problems.

Many people are surprised to hear the recommendation that they feed their adult Shih Tzu twice a day. For years, most people fed their dogs once daily. However, most veterinarians now recommend twice daily feedings, especially for small dogs (and very large dogs). Your Shih Tzu digests and absorbs his food better if he has two small

Young puppies should be fed four times a day. Adults should get two meals a day for optimal health.

meals, instead of one larger meal. Also, toy dogs, especially as puppies, have a tendency to develop *hypoglycemia*, also known as low blood sugar. While some puppies grow out of this condition, for a few dogs it's a chronic problem. More frequent meals help to keep blood sugar levels more even throughout the day.

Meals Versus Free Feeding

It's tempting to leave a bowl of food out for your Shih Tzu and let him decide when he wants to eat. It's not a good idea. Here are a few reasons why regular meals rather than free feeding is good for your Shih Tzu:

- **Shih Tzu tend to love their food—too much.** It's important for your dog's health to keep him slim and trim. If he decides how much he's going to eat, chances are great you'll have a chubby Shih Tzu. Fat dogs live fewer years than do their slimmer counterparts.
- **Monitoring how much your dog eats at his meals may be your first clue that he's sick.** If your dog usually licks the last morsel from his bowl, but then begins to pick at his meals for a day or so, it's a good idea to check with your veterinarian. This is much harder to notice if you free-feed your dog. In homes with more than one dog, it's impossible to know if one of them is skipping meals unless you feed them regularly.
- **Feeding meals improves your relationship with your dog.** Your sweet-eyed, round-faced, snubbed-nosed Shih Tzu certainly doesn't look like a wolf, but he shares his wolf ancestor's view of who runs the pack. In his view, whoever decides when and where meals take place is in charge of

the pack. When he is allowed to free-feed, he thinks he runs the house. When you provide regular meals, he thinks you're the alpha wolf. Dogs listen to the one who controls the food.

- **Your dog will behave better when he gets regular meals instead of free feeding.** Because he sees you as being the one in charge, a shy dog will become more confident. Bossy dogs become more compliant. Shih Tzu can be independent little dogs; feeding meals will help bond the two of you and will make your dog more likely to do what you ask of him.
- **Regular meals help with housetraining.** Regular meals mean regular potty times. You'll know when he's likely to need to go outside. This is a big plus in a breed notorious for being difficult to housetrain!

Shih Tzu Feeding Schedule

Until 3 Months Old: Four times a day
For example: 6:00 am, 10:00 am, 2:00 pm, and 6:00 pm

3 to 6 Months: Three times a day
For example: 6:00 am, noon, and 6:00 pm

Six months and older: Twice a day
For example: 6:00 am and 6:00 pm

Senior dog: May go back to three meals a day

HOW MUCH TO FEED

If you've always had to struggle with your weight, chances are you can relate to your Shih Tzu! Sturdily built dogs like Shih Tzu tend to put on weight easily, so it's important not to overfeed your little buddy.

Two different dogs of the same size may need different amounts of food. It depends on their age, energy level, exercise level, and metabolism.

Before you bring your dog home, ask the breeder or rescue group how much your dog normally eats at every meal. If you receive a vague answer (such as "about a handful"), ask to be shown exactly what that means. Keep an eye on your Shih Tzu. If he starts getting a bit tubby, slightly reduce how much you're feeding him. If he gets a tad thin, give him just a smidgen more.

Remember: Shih Tzu don't require a lot of food, because they are relatively small dogs. The biggest mistake most people make is overfeeding a Shih Tzu, not underfeeding him.

The Finicky Eater

Although most Shih Tzu love their meals, a few pick at their

If your Shih Tzu is a fussy eater, discuss his health and your options with your veterinarian.

food. They'll look at their food, give you that sad and soulful look, and walk away. Or they'll lie down and stare at it, as if they are *so* disappointed you didn't do a better job. Some turn up their noses until you bring them something that meets their standards—like steak.

Picky eaters aren't getting all the nutrition they need. A balanced diet, given in appropriate amounts, is essential to keeping a healthy immune system.

If you have a picky eater, talk with your veterinarian. A poor appetite can be a sign that your dog is sick. If your veterinarian agrees that you have a healthy dog who is just trying to wheedle his way into tasty tidbits instead of balanced food, the answer is to keep to your meal plan. Put down his dish. If he doesn't eat his dinner, take the food up and don't give him anything (no snacks, no bites from the table) until his next mealtime. Start again with fresh food for the next meal, and leave it out for 20 minutes. If he doesn't eat, take it away (again—so snacks or tidbits!). By the third mealtime, almost every Shih Tzu on the face of the earth will dive into his food.

Only skip meals with adult dogs. Puppies shouldn't skip meals.

WHERE TO FEED

Feed your Shih Tzu his meals in his crate. The crate offers a quiet, safe place where your dog can relax while he eats. It also reminds him that his crate is a great place.

If you have more than one dog, make sure each dog has his own bowl and eats his own food. You don't want them stealing each other's food at mealtime—a habit that can turn friends into enemies. Better yet, feed each dog in his crate. This gives each Shih Tzu a safe place in which to finish an uninterrupted meal.

WHAT TO FEED

Go to a major pet supply store, and you can find yourself reeling from the overwhelming number of choices. It's not unusual to find more than 150 brands, varieties, and flavors of dog food at one of the pet super stores. It's too much to absorb. The trick is to break down the choices available to you so that you can decide which dog food makes the most sense for you and your dog.

Everyone agrees on one point: Quality counts! It's extremely important to feed your Shih Tzu the best food you can afford. Depending on your little guy's size and metabolism, he could be eating as little as a ½ cup of food per day. Even a few mouthfuls of doggy junk food can have a serious impact on your dog's nutrition. Feeding your dog the right food, in the right amounts, is one of the best things you can do for your Shih Tzu. Select a food that has quality ingredients. It will make a difference in the life of your dog.

Commercial Dog Foods

Most Shih Tzu eat commercial dog food. The first thing to look for is the statement from the Association of American Feed Control Officials (AAFCO) on the label, which states that the food has met the organization's standards for the right mix of such things as protein, fats, and vitamins. The AAFCO guidelines are only a starting point, however. Surprisingly, these guidelines don't guarantee the products used in the food are absorbable by your pet's digestive system. In fact, one pet food company once demonstrated this point by concocting a "food" that met the AAFCO standards with ingredients like old shoe leather and crank case oil! This "food" was just a demonstration, but it makes one thing clear: Before you buy food for your Shih Tzu, check the ingredients.

It's not like your Shih

Feeding a high-quality food will result in a healthier Shih Tzu.

Leaders Ask Their Dogs to Earn Their Dinners

Before you put your dog's meal down, ask him to do something simple: sit, lie down, or do a trick he likes to do. This reinforces your role as the gentle and kind but strong leader of the Shih Tzu pack.

Do the same when you give your dog a treat. Ask him to earn it. This reinforces his obedience training, and he will be a calmer, more content dog because, in his eyes, you are acting like a competent leader.

Tzu eats as much as a Labrador or Newfoundland, so spend the few extra pennies to purchase a premium brand food for your dog. Premium brands aren't usually for sale in grocery stores. You'll find them at pet supply stores or at your veterinarian's office.

Compare labels. You'll soon notice that premium brands have meat listed as one of the first few ingredients. Lesser grades of dog food often have ingredients such as soy, wheat, corn, or beet pulp near the top of the list. Don't buy dog foods that use by-products or meal as their primary source of protein. The real deal—plain old chicken or beef—is better.

Dry Food

Feeding dry food can help with one of the biggest problems faced by Shih Tzu—dental problems. This breed has more dental problems than do most other breeds. Although feeding kibble isn't a cure-all to the problem, kibble can help somewhat to keep tartar accumulation under control. Feeding a diet of soft food makes the breed's already significant dental problems worse.

Buy a premium-brand kibble that contains good-quality ingredients. Experiment with the size and shape of kibble to see what your dog prefers—several brands have smaller nuggets for smaller dogs. Some are also specially designed dental formulas that your veterinarian can recommend.

Your dog doesn't eat a lot, so it's possible for dry food to become stale and even rancid. Put your nose in the bag periodically. It should smell like fresh biscuits. If the odor has changed, it's time for a new bag. Keeping kibble in the freezer will lengthen its shelf life.

Semi-Moist and Canned Food

Canned and semi-moist brands of food can be convenient, and many dogs prefer their taste to kibble. However, they have one big drawback: They make dental problems worse. The kibble scrapes against the teeth, helping reduce tartar. Soft foods stick to the teeth and actually promote tartar buildup. If you choose a soft food, be sure to brush your Shih Tzu's teeth daily. Also, give him toys to chew that will help "floss" his teeth.

Do be aware that, to maintain the soft texture, many semi-moist foods contain high quantities of preservatives. If you're

Although growing puppies are sometimes fed together, it is best for each dog in the family to have his own bowl and be monitored to be sure they're eating enough.

concerned about your dog ingesting chemicals, examine the ingredients carefully.

Whether you're feeding canned, semi-moist, or dry, what matters most is the quality of the ingredients. Always select brands that offer the most nutrition for your little buddy.

Chemical-Free Foods

Americans are becoming more nutrition-minded than ever before. That concern for healthy food choices extends to our pets. The result is a big increase in the sale of more natural, wholesome dog foods. Many brands now only use ingredients that pass federal inspections for human food. (These brands advertise "human grade" or "USDA-inspected meats" on their packaging.) A few brands have gone a step further and only use organic ingredients.

A growing number of pet supply stores feature wholesome foods. Some grocery store chains that specialize in health foods now stock several brands of premium, all-natural dog food.

Alternatives to Chemical Preservatives

People who are increasingly wary about chemicals in their own food would be surprised to look at the labels on traditional

It Pays to Read the Label

Advertisers are beginning to figure out that you want your pet to eat more natural food, but sometimes the reality is different from the hype. One dog food brand comes to mind. The TV advertising touts wholesome ingredients like peas and carrots. The bag design has pictures of meats and veggies—plus colorful photos of brightly colored kibble.

Read the label, and you'll be surprised. The food does contain peas and carrots, but in smaller quantities than a long list of other ingredients, including corn gluten meal, various animal by-products, sugar, and a chemical preservative. That bright coloring for the kibble came from yellow dyes number 5 and 6, red dye number 40, and blue dye number 2.

Always read the ingredients. Sometimes it pays to be cynical.

dog food brands. Most pet foods in the United States have depended on preservatives to give them a long shelf life. Common additives have been BHA, BHT, or ethoxyquin. A lot of controversy has surfaced about these additives, because some concern exists that (in certain quantities) they can cause cancer.

For people who want a more natural approach to pet food, increasing numbers of brands use natural alternatives to chemical preservatives. Many dog foods are now preserved with "mixed tocopherols" (vitamin E). Just 10 years ago, it was hard to find brands that avoided chemical preservatives. However, dog food companies have noticed consumers' preferences for naturally preserved food, and even major manufacturers are switching to more natural ingredients (or offering more natural product lines).

Because brands that use alternative, less toxic preservatives are now widely available, why not select those for your Shih Tzu?

The Cost of Natural Ingredients

More natural usually translates into more money out of your pocket. Super-premium food with human-grade ingredients can cost two to three times more than do grocery store brands. Still, knowing that your dog is getting good-quality ingredients is worth the cost to many Shih Tzu lovers. One of the advantages of having a small dog is that he doesn't eat much—so feeding him the very best foods doesn't have to stretch your wallet.

Home-Cooked Meals

Lots of dog owners are giving up entirely on commercial food and cooking their own food. If you're considering cooking for your Shih Tzu, proceed with real caution. Home-cooked meals can have the benefit of fresh, wholesome ingredients, but they can have the downside of providing your dog with inadequate nutrition. Done wrong, home cooking can do far more harm than good.

Dogs and humans have different nutritional needs. It's not enough to share your dinner with your dog. Plenty of research has been done to determine the mix of carbohydrates, proteins, and fats dogs need. Some excellent doggy cookbooks use this scientific information to give excellent recipes that provide balanced nutrition for your dog. However, other cookbooks reportedly have recipes that don't include the necessary range of nutrients to keep your Shih Tzu healthy.

Check with your veterinarian before deciding to cook for your dog. Make sure that you select meal plans that meet all your dog's needs.

Raw Foods

The most controversial diets include raw meat as part of the food plan. Many people who feed their dogs raw meat say they see major health improvements in their dogs. They cite shinier coats and improvements in health conditions from allergies to digestive upsets.

Skeptics, on the other hand, worry about microbes in raw meat, including *Salmonella* and *Escherichia coli*. People who believe in the health benefits of raw meat argue that a dog's digestive tract is designed to handle raw meat.

If you decide to try a raw food diet, do your research. There's a lot more to it than giving your dog uncooked steak! Correctly done, this diet includes pulverized vegetables as well as enzymes. If you only feed your dog raw meat, he'll quickly end up undernourished or even sick.

Several books on the market explain how to correctly feed a raw diet and provide recipes for raw meals for dogs.

If you like the idea of a raw food diet but are concerned

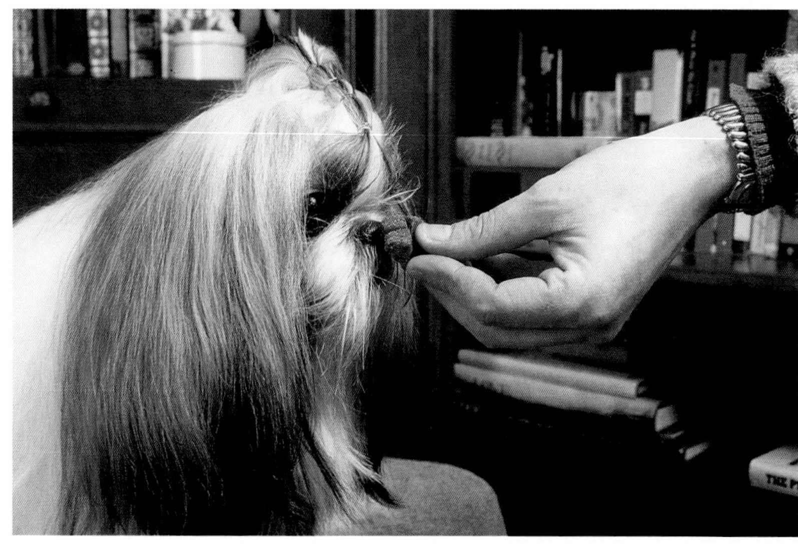

Raw foods that have been frozen and packaged are convenient to feed as meals or treats.

Time for a Change?

Is your Shih Tzu's coat shiny and silky? Is his skin supple? Is he free of itching and dryness? Are his eyes free of watering or discharge? Are his stools firm? If your dog looks exceptionally healthy, it's probably not worth considering a diet change.

If he doesn't look quite as vibrant as he might, it could be time to think about a new brand of dog food.

about concocting one that meets your dog's nutritional needs, consider purchasing one of the brands of frozen raw food. You'll find these in the freezer section of some specialty pet supply stores (usually those focusing on more natural products) and even in the frozen section of small health food stores.

Frozen raw foods are convenient—you keep the food in your freezer and thaw a portion shortly before your dog's meal. These meals meet the AAFCO nutrition requirements, so you know your dog is getting everything he needs in his food.

Frozen raw food is the most expensive option for feeding your dog. Still, your Shih Tzu doesn't eat a lot, so the cost of switching to even the most expensive frozen raw food is fairly minimal.

Some brands are frozen into small cubes or medallions, while others are frozen into larger loaves or "chubs." It's easiest to defrost a medallion or a couple of cubes—defrosting larger loaves or chipping away at a frozen loaf to get a Shih Tzu-sized meal can be a little frustrating.

You must follow the same strict hygiene with raw dog food that you follow any time you handle raw meat. Only feed your dog freshly defrosted food—throw away food if it's been in the refrigerator more than a couple days. Give your dog his dinner—and throw away anything he hasn't eaten within 20 minutes. (Chances are he'll gobble up the raw food in seconds, though!)

Wash bowls, countertops, and everything else that touches the raw food thoroughly with soap and water. Wash your hands carefully after handling the raw food. (Remember the old trick of singing "Happy Birthday" to yourself twice—that's how long it takes to thoroughly wash your hands.)

It's always best to work with your veterinarian in whatever food choices you make for your dog. Raw food is no exception. However, some veterinarians support feeding raw, others are neutral, and others oppose it. If you are strongly committed to feeding a raw diet, find a veterinarian who shares your philosophy, so you can get the kind of advice that's helpful to you. (A more holistic veterinarian may agree with your philosophy on other issues as well, if a more natural approach to living is a priority for you.)

Is raw food just a fad or a major revolution in the way we

feed our dogs? The next few years will determine that.

Puppies have so much to adapt to when they come to a new home that it is best to continue to feed what the breeder or seller has been feeding. Make dietary changes gradually.

Special Diets

Prescription diets are available for a wide variety of conditions, including kidney problems, allergies, and dental issues. Several pet food companies provide prescription diets, so you and your veterinarian can choose among them. Your veterinarian may also give you instructions for a home-cooked diet if your dog has special needs.

This is a time to listen to your veterinarian—and not the self-appointed "experts" who seem to hang out on every Internet chat group for dog lovers. The Internet can be a good place to get general information about dogs and Shih Tzu. However, it makes no sense to take diet advice from perfect strangers who have never met your dog.

Shih Tzu have more than their fair share of allergies. If your dog is one of them, your veterinarian may recommend an *elimination diet*. On these programs, the dog is given a meal that only has two or three ingredients. Usually, the protein is something the dog has never been exposed to. It might be something as exotic as ostrich or kangaroo meat. Gradually, additional ingredients are added one at a time, so the veterinarian can identify which foods trigger your Shih Tzu's allergies.

Supplements

Research over the past few years has shown that some additives can help dogs stay healthy. For example, fatty acids from fish oil can aid digestion, improve coat, and help with allergies. Studies have shown that glucosamine and chondroitin sulfate can keep joints healthy, which can be important if your Shih Tzu has hip dysplasia.

Be careful about supplements, however. Too much of a good thing isn't good. Discuss any supplements with your

Changing Food

Want to avoid tummy upsets? Want to ensure that your Shih Tzu doesn't go on a hunger strike? Then make all food changes gradually. Take a week to transition from one brand to another, gradually increasing the amount of new food and decreasing the amount of old food each day.

veterinarian. Don't give your dog any vitamins without discussing them with your veterinarian. Some vitamins are toxic at high levels.

Bones

One of the most deadly mistakes that dog owners make is to give their dogs cooked bones. Cooking—even for just a couple of minutes—changes the structure of a bone, making it sharp and splintery. While all cooked bones are dangerous, chicken and turkey bones are the worst. These sharp bones can rip through your dog's stomach and intestines. It's just as dangerous as giving your little dog a sharp knife as a toy!

If your dog accidentally eats a cooked bone, call your veterinarian right away for advice.

Raw bones, on the other hand can be a healthy treat for your dog. Chewing on a raw bone can help clean your Shih Tzu's teeth.

Feeding raw bones still requires your supervision. Be careful that you aren't giving bones (such as some marrow bones) that are small enough to get lodged in your dog's throat.

Remember, raw bones can leave a Shih Tzu's coat smelling like dead meat—so this is a treat best given just before your dog's scheduled bath!

Treats

People who eat too much ice cream or too many french fries aren't healthy. Dogs who get too many treats aren't healthy, either.

Don't thoughtlessly hand your dog treats all the time. When you give him treats, make it good quality food, such as a tidbit of lean meat. Never give him hot dogs or other food full of salt and chemicals. You might be surprised that most Shih Tzu love veggies, so your treats can be little bits of carrots or tomatoes. Keep the portions tiny. After all, a Shih Tzu is a small dog. Instead of giving him a large piece of meat or doggy treat, make his treat the size of a pencil eraser. He gets the treat he enjoys without overly expanding his waistline.

Modern obedience training is based on the joys of working for food. You don't have to turn your Shih Tzu into a tank to train him! Keep those training treats, like other treats, tiny and healthful.

It's always tempting to give your buddy extra treats—he won't say no! It's up to you to monitor his food intake for his long-term health.

Remember, food rewards are for a job well done, not for begging at the table!

FEEDING YOUR PUPPY

Adjusting to a new home is hard enough—don't switch your new puppy's food too soon. Your Shih Tzu puppy should stay on the same diet and be fed at the same times for at least a week before you make any changes.

To give your puppy the best start in his new home:

- Purchase the puppy's food before you bring him home. You don't want to be running to the store when you have a hungry puppy on your hands.
- Get instructions from the breeder ahead of time that tell you how much, how often, and when the puppy eats.
- Ask your veterinarian if the puppy's diet is ideal. Most veterinarians recommend feeding a premium-quality food formulated specifically for puppies during their first year.
- If your veterinarian recommends a different food, don't make sudden changes. Keep the puppy on his original food for at least a week. If you want to make a change after that time, gradually add a little of the new food in with the old, switching your puppy to his new food over a period of several days.

Senior Shih Tzu have special needs. They may benefit from more frequent but smaller meals, and because of their dental problems, may need softer food.

FEEDING YOUR SENIOR SHIH TZU

A good diet is important throughout our lives. It's most important as we get older and the aging process begins to take its toll. The same is true for our dogs. When your Shih Tzu hits middle age—about 7 or 8 years old—it's time to ask your veterinarian if you should be adjusting his diet a bit.

Your veterinarian may want to run some blood tests to see how your dog's organs are doing. It's not unusual for older dogs to be a bit deficient in their kidney or liver functions, or to have some mild heart problems. If your veterinarian finds some of these issues, she might suggest a prescription diet.

Older dogs, like older people, tend to gain weight more easily, so your veterinarian may suggest reduced portions or a different dog food.

As long as your senior Shih Tzu is a healthy dog, your veterinarian will probably recommend that you continue to do just what you have been doing.

Dental disease is a problem in Shih Tzu; many have lost several teeth by the time they're senior-canine citizens. Make sure your dog can comfortably eat what you are feeding him. It might be a good idea to feed him smaller-sized kibbles or moisten his food.

Some oldsters become finicky eaters. It's more important than ever for your old guy to get complete nutrition, so do what you can to make his food tasty. Try warming moist foods a little in the microwave. You can mix tiny portions of yummy treats, such as lean meat, into his food. (Be careful not to find yourself gradually changing his diet to doggy junk food, though.) Some older dogs do better on three smaller meals rather than two larger ones, because it allows them to absorb the nutrition better.

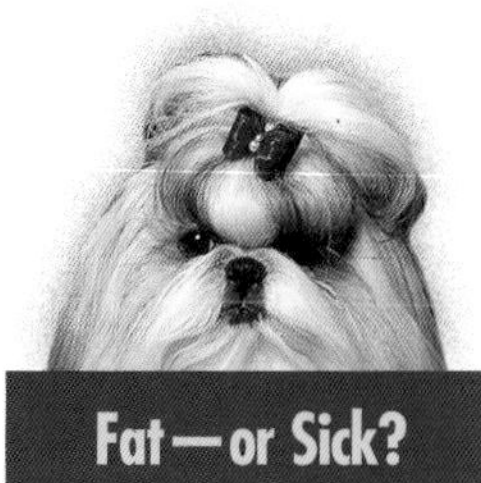

Fat—or Sick?

When you see a Shih Tzu with a round tummy, chances are he's just eating too much. However, sometimes that tummy is a sign of a health problem.

Shih Tzu have a tendency to develop thyroid problems. Dogs with low thyroid levels gain weight. If your dog is on a low-calorie diet and isn't losing weight, have his thyroid levels checked. If thyroid dysfunction is the problem, he can receive medication and go back to his slender self.

If your dog is slender except for a swollen abdomen, that's also a sign of a health problem. The problem might be a case of puppy worms, which is easily treated. Or, it might be as serious as fluids accumulating in your dog's abdomen, which will be fatal if you don't get your dog immediate medical attention. See your veterinarian right away if your dog's abdomen swells over a short period of time.

THE CHUBBY SHIH TZU

The biggest health risk to your Shih Tzu comes from you. Shih Tzu love snacks and have a tendency to gain weight. It's no wonder so many are pudgy little pooches.

How much difference does it make to keep your dog slender? In a study completed by Purina, slender dogs lived almost 2 years longer than did those who were just a little bit heavier.

This study tracked a group of 48 Labrador Retrievers throughout their lifetimes. Half free-fed and ate what they wanted to; the other half was fed 25 percent less than the free-feeders. Here's the difference that reduction of calories made:

- The median life span for the control group (free-fed dogs) was 11.2 years; it was 13 years for the lean dogs.
- By age 10, 7 of the 24 control group dogs had died—and only 3 lean dogs had died.
- At age 12, only 1 control group dog was still alive—but 11 lean dogs were still alive.
- None of the control group dogs lived to be 13 and a half—but 25 percent of the lean dogs did.

No doubt about it: If you want your Shih Tzu to live a long life, you need to keep him slim and trim.

But there's another reason to keep your little buddy slender: Not only will he live longer, he'll be healthier and happier, too. The fact is that weight makes other health problems worse. For example, if your Shih Tzu has hip dysplasia, he'll be in more pain if he's overweight. If he has conditions such as heart disease, kidney problems, or liver disease, all those organs have

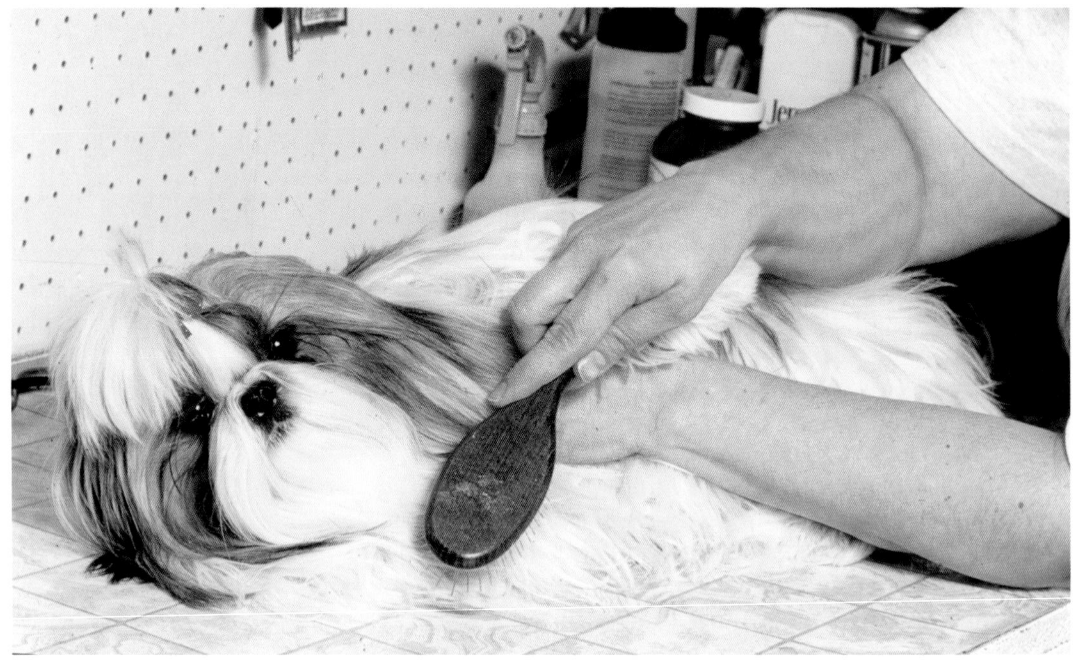

Grooming sessions are excellent times to feel your dog all over for signs of injury or potential illness—including weight gain.

to work harder if he's carrying extra weight.

New research indicates that substances in fat actually cause inflammation. So, if your dog is overweight, the fat actually causes his joints to hurt more. Since many Shih Tzu have joint problems, it's especially important to keep the weight down.

Your slender dog will want to do more things with you. He'll want to play more, go for more walks, and have more fun. These wonderful dogs are only on earth for a limited time—make every day count!

Checking Your Shih Tzu's Weight

Shih Tzu are naturally sturdy little dogs. You don't want your dog to have the build of a Greyhound. Still, when your dog is at the right weight, you'll be able to feel the outline of his ribs under your fingers. If you stand over him, you should see a definite indentation at his waistline. You can feel a tuck-up on his tummy behind his ribs.

If your dog is chubby, you won't see a waistline. Maybe you can feel the ribs—if you poke through a layer of fat. His belly will be round instead of lean.

Of course you love your dog, no matter whether he's chubby or slim. But because you love him, help him be slender and fit.

Remember, by watching what he eats, you're adding the probability of 2 extra years to spend together! That's worth giving up a few doggy biscuits for!

Losing Weight

Dieting for dogs is just like dieting for people: Eat less and exercise more. If your Shih Tzu is just a little bit overweight, cut down on his snacks and add a walk or play session to his day. Most likely, he'll lose the weight he needs to. If that isn't enough, develop a diet plan with his veterinarian.

Some "light" foods are on the market, but most likely your veterinarian will suggest reducing the amount of your dog's regular food. You can also ask your veterinarian about adding some tasty, low-calorie goodies to your dog's food to make him feel full without getting fat. Two foods that are often added are green beans and pumpkin—they add volume without increasing calories.

Your dog doesn't have to give up snacks while he's on a diet. Just switch to wholesome snacks. You'd be surprised how many dogs love little pieces of carrots or dried sweet potatoes.

FOODS TO AVOID

Foods that are perfectly healthy for humans can make your dog seriously ill—and might even kill him. Because Shih Tzu are small dogs, a small amount of these foods can cause irreparable harm to your best buddy.

Here is a partial list of foods that should never, ever cross your Shih Tzu's lips:

- **Grapes and raisins.** In the last few years, even veterinarians were surprised to learn that these snacks are deadly to many dogs. In many cases, just a handful of raisins or grapes caused kidney failure in some

The right food and healthy treats are critical to your Shih Tzu's health, as are sufficient exercise, grooming, and attention.

Your Shih Tzu will thrive on a balanced diet.

dogs. No one understands why they are so dangerous, and no one knows why some dogs have eaten them and been perfectly fine while others went into acute kidney failure. If your dog eats grapes or raisins, call your veterinarian right away.

- **Chocolate.** Chocolate is just an overindulgence for humans. It's a toxin for dogs. Many dogs like the taste of chocolate, so be sure to keep chocolate away from any place your curious Shih Tzu can climb. The darker chocolates have the highest concentration of dangerous substances, but milk chocolate can still make your dog sick. Gardeners beware: Cocoa bean shells are a popular mulch in some areas—and they contain the same toxins as chocolate for dogs.

- **Coffee.** Drinking coffee can lead to serious heart and neurological problems for your Shih Tzu. Many dogs like the taste of coffee, so be sure to keep your latte, coffee beans, and coffee grounds out of your dog's reach.
- **Alcoholic beverages.** A very small amount of alcohol can cause alcohol poisoning in your dog. It's never humorous or clever to give a dog even a drop of alcohol.
- **Avocados.** This is another food that seems healthy but can kill a dog. The toxic component is called persin. The toxic dose isn't known, so don't let your Shih Tzu eat any amount of avocado.
- **Macadamia nuts.** No one knows why macadamia nuts—a healthy snack for humans—are so toxic to dogs. We do know that as few as six nuts can kill a dog.
- **Moldy food.** While some molds are harmless, others cause neurological problems in some dogs. Keep the dog out of the garbage and away from moldy foods.
- **Onions.** Onions cause severe anemia in dogs. Garlic can have the same effect, but dogs rarely eat enough garlic to cause a substantial problem. The good news is that anemia caused by onions or garlic will go away once the dog stops eating these foods.
- **Yeast dough.** It's tempting to give your Shih Tzu just a smidgen of dough while you're cooking. Don't. Raw dough will "rise" in his stomach, dangerously stretching and expanding it. Alcohol is also produced when the dough "rises" and can create alcohol poisoning in your Shih Tzu. This is more of a problem in small breeds (such as Shih Tzu) than in larger ones.

You love your Shih Tzu and would do anything for him. Of all the gifts you can give him, a lean, healthy, balanced diet is the most important. Purchase the very best food for him, and don't overfeed him.

If you feed your Shih Tzu right, years will be added to his life, and he will better enjoy his time with you. What could be more important than that?

Call for Help

Not all toxic poisonings are treated the same. Sometimes it's best to have the dog throw up—other times that's the worst treatment. Sometimes you can take a "wait and see" approach, but at other times immediate care at an emergency clinic will save your dog's life. Ask an expert to find out the right thing to do for your little guy.

If your Shih Tzu has eaten something that might be toxic (see the list "Foods to Avoid"), call your veterinarian or emergency clinic right away. You can also call the ASPCA Animal Poison Control Center, which is staffed 24 hours a day, 365 days a year. These experts charge a phone consultation fee, but that call might save your dog's life. The toll-free number is (888) 426-4435.

Chapter 5

GROOMING
Your Shih Tzu

Shih Tzu are charming. They're intelligent. They're loving. They're adorable.

But mostly, they are hairy. These dogs have hair on their muzzles that will grow to the ground if you don't trim it. They have fur that will follow them like a bridal train. Although all that hair can be gorgeous, it is also a huge responsibility to maintain. Although it's easier to care for a Shih Tzu who's cut down in a comfy pet clip (rather than one who has the long tresses of a show dog), every Shih Tzu needs regular grooming to be comfortable.

While coat care is an obvious concern when you groom your Shih Tzu, a dog lives underneath all that hair—and that means cleaning ears, caring for teeth, and trimming his toenails.

This chapter will help you keep your Shih Tzu looking and feeling terrific!

PREPARING YOUR SHIH TZU TO LOVE GROOMING

Shih Tzu are combed, clipped, and coifed. They have to be comfortable and patient with sometimes daily brushing, frequent baths, and regular trips to the groomer. And, as with every other dog, your Shih Tzu needs regular teeth cleaning, nail trimming, and general maintenance. This all adds up to a good portion of your dog's life being spent in grooming and care.

Whether those are happy hours or miserable ones is up to you. If you teach your little dog to associate grooming with treats, attention, and love, he'll look forward to it. If you treat grooming as a grim task—or worse yet, put it off until he's in such bad shape that grooming is mostly about pulling out tangled knots—your dog will spend a lot of his life in fear and pain.

Happily, it's pretty easy to teach your dog to enjoy his grooming regimen.

Get your Shih Tzu used to the grooming process by starting him as a puppy on a grooming table.

Where to Groom

Little dogs aren't groomed on the floor. They're groomed on laps and on tables, and they're bathed in sinks. That means most of your dog's grooming time is spent up in the air.

Just think of those heights from your little guy's perspective. Lifting your Shih Tzu up on to a table is the equivalent of you being plucked by a crane and hoisted onto the top of a three-story building. It's no wonder that a lot of dogs run away when it's time to be groomed. The whole experience starts with the scary experience of being hoisted into the air! Before you can expect your dog to be comfortable when you groom him, you must teach him that it's okay to be lifted up and put on a table.

Teach Lift Up

Several times a day, gently pick up your Shih Tzu and hold him for just a moment. Be careful to hold his body comfortably. Say "Good lift up!," give him a treat, and put him gently down on the floor. Soon, "lift up" will be one of his favorite things to do.

Once he likes being picked up, you can practice putting him on the table or counter where you'll be grooming him and give him a treat. Make sure the surface isn't slippery. Always put down a mat or towel, so that your dog feels he's in a safe place with firm footing. The more often you place him on surfaces and give him treats, the more likely he'll be of accepting whatever procedures happen on those surfaces.

Hold Tight—but Hold Right

Picking up your Shih Tzu by holding him around the ribs and having his back legs dangling in the air can be painful for your dog. Always support his rear end and chest when you pick him up.

Teach Your Dog the Names of His Body Parts

Imagine going to your doctor and having her touch your most personal parts without telling you what's about to happen. Chances are, you wouldn't be happy at all.

That's just how grooming (and vet visits) feel to your dog. Without warning, someone grabs at his face or tail, or decides to clean his most intimate areas. It's no wonder dogs get grouchy.

Humans are able to accept all those extremely personal doctor's visits—not to mention hairdressers who tug at our tresses—because we know what's going to happen next. We prepare ourselves physically and mentally.

You can teach your Shih Tzu the names of his body parts by saying them when you're working on them. This puppy learns "Good ear!"

You can help your dog prepare himself, as well. If you teach your Shih Tzu the names of his body parts, he'll be able to understand what's happening to him and calmly accept it.

It's easy and fun to teach your dog the names of his parts. Just touch your Shih Tzu's ear, say "Good ear!," and give him a treat. Do the same with "Good nose!" or "Good tail!" and all his other parts. Teach him names for his eyes, ears, feet, nose, tail, teeth, tummy, and rear end. Quickly, he'll think that being touched in specific places—even delicate ones—is a cause for celebration.

Once he knows the names of his body parts, up the ante a little bit. Hold his foot while you say "Good foot!" and reward him. Explore between his toes. Touch his muzzle, and then reward him when you gently open his mouth and teach him to accept having all his teeth touched.

If he struggles and pulls back, you're going too fast. Relax. Take your time. This is a game for the two of you. It's a bonding time. It's fun. When your dog enjoys having you touch him, ask friends to touch and reward him. Your dog will learn to love all the attention.

Imagine the difference this training will make when you're grooming your dog or taking him to a groomer or a veterinarian. When you tell him "Lift up," he'll be happy and relaxed when he gets on the table. He'll know what's happening, so he'll feel safe and secure.

This will change your dog's perspective of grooming from a scary, unpredictable time to a relaxing day at the spa. Both of you will be happier, more bonded, and more relaxed.

A Shih Tzu groomed for the show ring is an unforgettable sight.

SHIH TZU HAIR STYLES

Shih Tzu are very versatile when it comes to the way in which their hair can be styled. This section will help you find the hair style best suited to your furry friend.

The Show Coat

When you go to a dog show and see a mature champion Shih Tzu in full coat, the sight is unforgettable. The dog's hair is a flowing, glowing work of art. Every single hair is in place. The long coat spills onto the ground. The dog's head is crowned with a topknot, set off with a brilliant bow.

If you wonder if it takes a lot of work maintaining that coat, watch the Shih Tzu's handler. She is combing that dog every single second while the dog is in the show ring. The perfect hair of a Shih Tzu in the ring is a bit like the perfect coif of a human supermodel; it isn't a casual effort.

Few people find it worth the trouble to keep a pet Shih Tzu in full show coat. In fact, most show exhibitors happily cut their champions into a short pet clip the day the dog's show career is finished.

Pet Clips

Chances are, you'll have your dog in a pet clip. They can be every bit as attractive as the long coat, if you go to a great groomer. Most Shih Tzu sport three basic clips: the Cocker Spaniel clip, the Schnauzer clip, and the puppy clip. All these clips (and variations on these themes) keep your dog looking attractive and feeling comfortable, and they are relatively easy to care for. Depending on your dog, you'll have to go to the groomer for a trim about every month or so.

Most Shih Tzu lovers take their dogs to professional groomers. If you like to play with hair, go ahead and learn to clip your dog yourself. And if your attempts at clipping don't succeed, remember that hair grows back!

Cocker Spaniel Clip

In the Cocker Spaniel clip, the dog's face and head is trimmed. His back is shaved to give a sleek, easy-to-care-for look. The hair on his tail is kept long. The fur on his legs is kept moderately long—sometimes the hair on the sides is also kept

Grooming Supplies

Think ahead. You don't want to be looking for supplies while you have a wet Shih Tzu puppy in the sink! Have on hand:

- Blow dryer
- Comb
- Conditioner
- Nail clippers
- Nonskid mat for sink or tub
- Pin, slicker, and/or bristle brush
- Scissors to trim feet and tidy up coat
- Shampoo
- Towels

Even a Shih Tzu in a puppy clip can enjoy a topknot.

fairly long (creating what looks like a skirt). This cut reminds you of the beauty of the dog's long hair but requires only fairly minimal upkeep.

Schnauzer Clip

The Schnauzer clip is similar to the Cocker clip, except that the legs and tummy are clipped to a shorter length. This cut gives a neat, tidy, ready-to-go appearance.

Puppy Clip

The puppy clip cuts the fur all over the dog to an even length, which looks a bit like the cute puppy stage when your dog was a little mass of fluff.

The Topknot

If you keep your dog's coat long, you'll need to pull the hair on his head into a topknot. Some people who keep their dogs' fur trimmed short also put a small topknot on their dogs.

A topknot keeps the hair away from the Shih Tzu's delicate eyes. In the show ring, they're important in framing the dog's expression—and expression is one of the hallmarks of the breed. If you decide to show your Shih Tzu, you'll want to learn the fine art of creating the perfect topknot (which can mean using hairspray and doing some back-combing!) from your dog's breeder.

A topknot is adorable on a pet Shih Tzu, but remember, the ultimate purpose isn't just looking good. A topknot is needed to keep the long hair away from your Shih Tzu's eyes.

To give your Shih Tzu a topknot, gently gather the hair from above your dog's eyes and nose and as far back as the crown. Be sure not to pull the topknot too tightly. That can be very uncomfortable for your dog and may lead to hair loss.

The Shih Tzu topknot has a bit of a poof to it; experiment until you get the look you like. When you're done, secure the topknot with a latex band. (You can find bands that are less entangling than regular rubber bands at your groomer's, pet

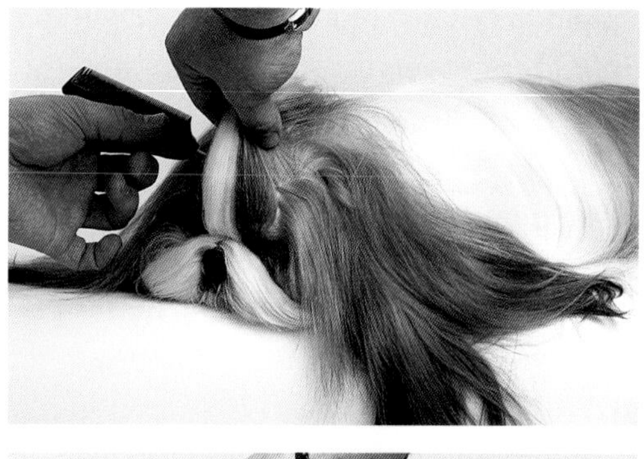

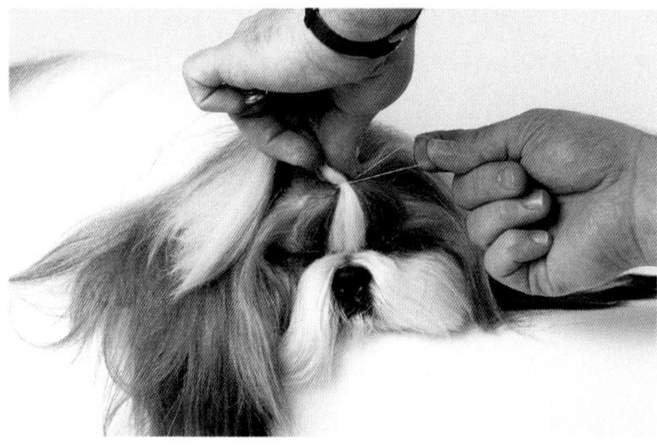

supply stores, or dog shows.)

Top off the topknot with a sparkling ribbon that complements your dog's coloring and brings out the brightness of his eyes. Some people braid the hair in the topknot, which also shows off the Shih Tzu's sweet expression and is an effective way to keep hair away from his eyes.

The Shih Tzu's topknot not only looks good, but it keeps the long hair out of the dog's eyes. It can be done by combing a section of hair, securing it with a rubber band, and finishing it off with a special bow.

COAT CARE

Even if you go to a professional groomer, your Shih Tzu's coat will still take a lot of commitment from you.

Shih Tzu have a double coat: a harsher outer layer and a wooly undercoat. The undercoat grows in and sheds every year. When the undercoat tangles in the outer coat, you're dog has a mat. He can also get mats in any area where skin and hair rub together, like under the elbows, behind the ears, and even along the tail.

You love your Shih Tzu and would never hurt him. But if you let mats develop in his coat, you are causing him excruciating pain. When your Shih Tzu has a mat on his tummy, it hurts to stretch out and sleep. If your dog has mats on his legs, it hurts to walk.

Brushing Tip

To keep the hair from breaking, don't ever brush or comb your dog's dry coat. Spritz his hair with water or a conditioning spray, then brush.

Can you imagine how terrible it would be to have every step hurt? Imagine how sad it is for your little dog to pull away from your touch—because his skin hurts from being pulled tight by mats. Your sweet Shih Tzu might even growl or bite at you because it hurts when you pet him.

Keep up on your dog's grooming so that he doesn't have to live in misery.

Start With Your Puppy

The best time to start combing and grooming all that hair is before it grows long. Your puppy's fuzzy coat usually doesn't tangle. That's the best time to teach him that brushes and combs feel good.

Although adult coats need a pin brush to navigate through the hair, you can start out with a soft brush on your puppy. Gently brush him all over: back, tummy, feet, tail, and head. Give him treats. Tell him he's handsome! Make it a little party! He'll look forward to grooming instead of fearing it.

Not tending to a Shih Tzu's coat can cause matting, dirt accumulation, and even health issues.

Brushing Your Shih Tzu

Whatever the length of your dog's coat, brush *and* comb him at least once a week. Different Shih Tzu have different coat textures. Some Shih Tzu, even in a short trim, need combing every day.

Start with a brush that is strong enough to get into the coat, but soft enough to be gentle on your dog's skin. Pin brushes, slickers, and boar-bristle brushes all have their proponents. Find what works best for you and your dog.

Be sure to brush all over your dog's body—not just the back and sides. Brush his tummy, the insides of his legs, under his tail—everywhere. It's those hidden places that are likely to develop the worst mats if you're not careful. Brush—then comb—every single hair on his body.

If your Shih Tzu has a long coat,

brush one layer at a time. Separate the coat into sections, working from the tummy up to the top. Be sure to brush clear down to the skin and not just the top of the hair. (Most show Shih Tzu are trained to lie quietly on a table while they are brushed, so they're relaxed and comfortable during this time-consuming process.)

Remember three words when combing and brushing your Shih Tzu: Gentle, gentle, and gentle. If you see a mat, don't try to tug it out. Hold the hair between the mat and the dog's skin and tease it out gently, so you don't pull his skin. If your dog isn't destined for the show ring, snip out stubborn mats with scissors. One thing you can be sure of: Your Shih Tzu's hair will grow back after you cut it.

Pay special attention to the pads of his feet and behind his ears, both places where mats develop especially quickly. Of course, be especially gentle when grooming around his genital area.

After you've brushed every single hair on your dog, comb every single hair. You'll be surprised at how many tiny mats a brush can miss. By combing your dog, you can catch those mats before they become a serious problem.

Shih Tzu are called *chrysanthemum dogs* because of the flower-like look of the hair growth on their faces. That adorable little flower face needs special attention. Every day, brush out any bits of food that might have become attached to your Shih Tzu's

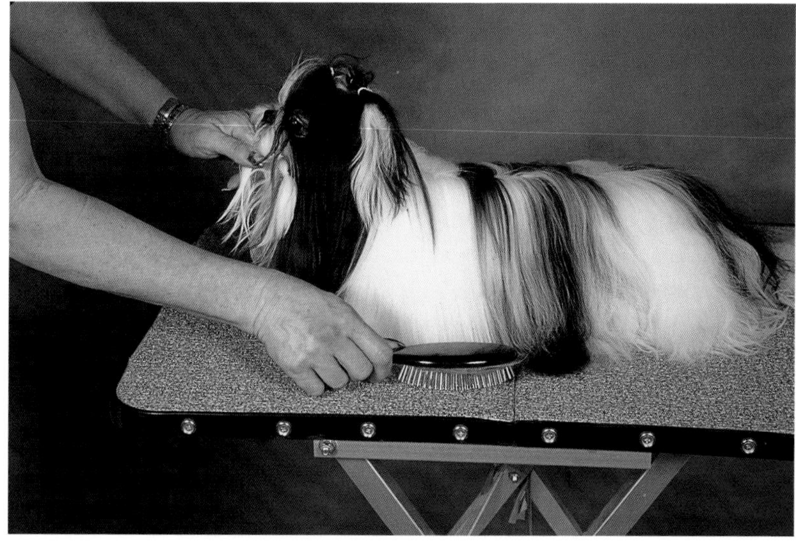

Your Shih Tzu's coat changes as he matures and loses his puppy fluff—another reason to be rigorous with regular grooming!

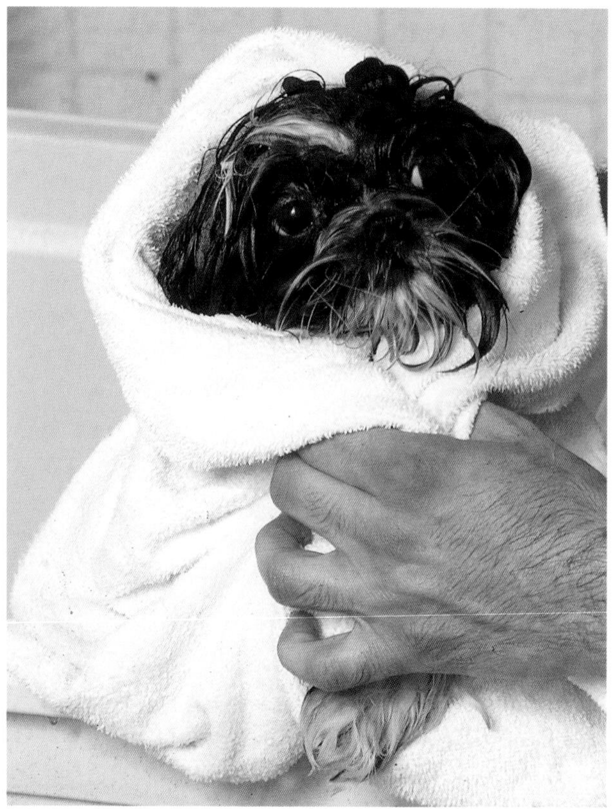

Your Shih Tzu should quickly become accustomed to a pleasant bath time.

muzzle. Wipe around his eyes with a damp cloth to keep his face clean of discharge. Some people use a very fine-toothed comb, such as a flea comb, to carefully comb out any discharge that still remains near the eyes.

Make grooming time your special time with your Shih Tzu. Sing to him—he'll never think you're off key. Laugh with him. Tell him he's the most gorgeous dog in the world. After all—he is!

The Great Puppy Shed

You might feel like you've been keeping up reasonably well with your Shih Tzu's grooming, then seemingly overnight your young dog is covered with mats. What happened?

The answer: puppy's first big shed. When your puppy is about 10 months old or so, he'll shed the last of his puppy fur while the new, adult coat grows in. This process takes about a month. Unhappily, that old coat is very likely to get caught in the new coat, creating mats that are miserable for your dog.

While your puppy is maturing, pay special attention to his coat and make sure to brush and comb him daily during this time.

Bathing Your Shih Tzu

Dirty coats mat much faster than do clean ones, so it's important to keep your Shih Tzu clean. Each dog varies in the accumulation of oils in his coat, but most Shih Tzu should be bathed about twice a month.

If you see this as a matter-of-fact, pleasant experience, so will your Shih Tzu. If you consider this a time for high drama—so will your dog. Be calm, focused, and efficient, and your dog will learn to tolerate his baths and maybe even enjoy them.

Remember this mantra for every longhaired dog breed: *Always thoroughly brush and comb your dog before you bathe him.* If you decide to cut corners, you will regret it. Once mats get wet, they get tighter and are harder to remove.

Yes, you will have to brush your dog, bathe him, and brush him again. Believe it or not, that's a lot less time-consuming and much easier for your dog than spending untold amounts of time trying to get tight mats out of your dog's coat. It will also be much more pleasant and less painful for your dog.

Most Shih Tzu fit easily in the sink. That's a real convenience, since it's a lot harder to bathe a dog when you have to stoop down and clean him in a tub. Put a non-skid mat in the sink, so your little guy has a firm footing. (The least expensive way to give him a firm footing is to purchase a rubber bath mat and cut it to fit your sink.) Be sure to put the drain filter in—it's scary for a little dog to find his paw slipping into the drain hole.

The water temperature should feel just slightly warm on your skin. Hot water can burn your dog's sensitive skin. And it's no fun for your dog if the water is too cold—a shivering Shih Tzu in a sink is not a happy sight.

Don't think of yourself as giving your Shih Tzu a bath—you are really giving him a shower. It's very helpful to have a hose attachment on your sink, so that you can direct the spray to thoroughly rinse all those tough-to-reach spots.

Choosing a shampoo for your Shih Tzu is just as personal as choosing one for yourself. Different dogs do well with different brands. Veterinarians and groomers usually have good-quality shampoos and conditioners for sale. Ask your breeder what brands she's had success with.

Gently massage the shampoo into your dog's hair and then rinse thoroughly. After you've rinsed out the shampoo, apply your dog's conditioner. Then rinse, and rinse again. Rinse one more time for good measure. Nothing makes a coat look duller—or makes skin feel itchier—than shampoo and conditioner left in a dog's coat after a bath.

Lift your dog out of the sink (you get to use his Lift Up command again) and place him on the counter, table, or grooming table where you'll dry him. Be sure he's on solid footing for drying. Put down a bath mat or towel so the surface feels safe and comfortable for your dog.

Dog Products Work Best

Most "people" shampoos will leave a dog's skin dry, itchy, and flaky, so use a good-quality shampoo formulated just for dogs.

Drying Your Shih Tzu

Start by completely towel-drying your Shih Tzu. Remember—don't rub or scrub at the hair—that will create mats! Gently squeeze the water out with the towel.

Brush and then comb out his hair. Be sure to get to all the areas that are easy to overlook, such as your dog's elbows, behind his ears, and his tummy.

If it's a warm summer day, and your dog is in a short clip, you can let him air dry after you've combed him out. However, most of the time, you'll want to blow dry your dog. The best choice for a dryer is one that's designed for dogs. The air doesn't ever get too hot to be safe for your dog. They're also convenient—some of them sit on your counter, leaving your hands free.

If you're using a human dryer, set the temperature to its lowest. A hot dryer can burn your dog's skin. Keep the volume on low as well—the air at full blast is unpleasant for your little guy, and he'll learn to resent his bath. You can also find stands to hold the hair dryer in place, so you will have both hands available to comb—always a good idea.

Always point the dryer in the direction you want your dog's hair to flow. Gently brush your dog as you dry him—brushing his coat in the same direction as the dryer points.

Most Shih Tzu learn to love the attention of their time at the "spa."

If you trim your Shih Tzu's nails, it's best to do them often. Holding him close to you keeps him secure.

Teach Your Shih Tzu to Accept the Dryer

Lots of dogs hate grooming because they're afraid of the blow dyer.

That shouldn't be surprising. After all, these contraptions are noisy and windy.

If your dog is afraid of the dryer, here's what to do:

- Leave the dryer in plain sight without turning it on. Reward your dog when he walks near it, so he begins to associate the dryer with treats.
- Hold the dryer (still on "off") with one hand, and pet your dog with your other

hand. Give him a treat, and tell him life is grand.

- Once the sight of the dryer doesn't scare your dog, turn the dryer on *while your dog is across the room*. Throw your dog a treat, and tell him he's brave.
- Gradually, throw treats shorter and shorter distances, until your dog happily takes treats from your hand while you're holding the running blow dryer.
- Make sure to always reward your dog at regular intervals when you're blow drying him—never let him forget that good things always happen near the contraption!

NAIL CARE

If you can hear your dog's nails clicking when he walks, with every step he takes, he's in pain. Your dog's nails are pushing into his feet when he puts his paw down—and that hurts.

When you take your Shih Tzu to the groomer for his regular haircut, always be sure she trims his nails. However, your monthly trip to the groomer isn't enough to keep your dog's nails short. Your dog's nails should be trimmed every week or two. You and your Shih Tzu can work out a system that's comfortable for both of you. Some people hold their dogs on their laps. You can either have the dog lying down on your lap, or standing and offering one paw at a time. Other people prefer a countertop or grooming table. Experiment to see what feels natural and makes you feel you have the control and vision you need to do the job of trimming your dog's nails.

If your Shih Tzu is a small one, you may be able to use cat nail clippers. These are easier for most people to control than the guillotine-style nail clippers; you can see exactly where you are trimming and can trim tiny amounts. Larger Shih Tzu will need one of the more traditional guillotine-style nail trimmers.

You must be careful when you trim your Shih Tzu's nails. Your dog has nerves and blood vessels that run down the center of his nail, called the quick. If you nick the quick, it hurts your dog and causes bleeding.

If you are very careful, your dog can go a lifetime without ever experiencing pain when you cut his nails. The secret is to snip only the very tip of your dog's nails.

If your dog's nails are very long, don't try to get to a short nail all at once. If you try, you are sure to hit the quick. Trim a

A Delicate Issue

Combine long hair and a dog's bodily functions, and you have the potential for a mess. In doggy circles, the result is known as a "cling-on." Groomers will tell you that they often see dogs whose rumps are a mass of dried excrement. This is an obvious health hazard for your little dog.

Teach your dog the command Let Me Check. Start out by giving him a treat with one hand while you run a tissue or paper towel across his rump with the other. If you spot a "cling-on," remove it. (This may require combing out or a quick rinsing in the sink. After you rinse your dog, be sure to clean the sink with a disinfecting cleanser, such as a water-bleach mixture.)

Your dog can get into a regular pattern of "let me check" every time he comes inside from a potty break, keeping him clean and giving you a chance to keep on top of this potentially serious problem.

You can also trim around a male's penis and a female's vulva, to reduce the accumulation of urine and urine stains. Rinse off those areas regularly, as well.

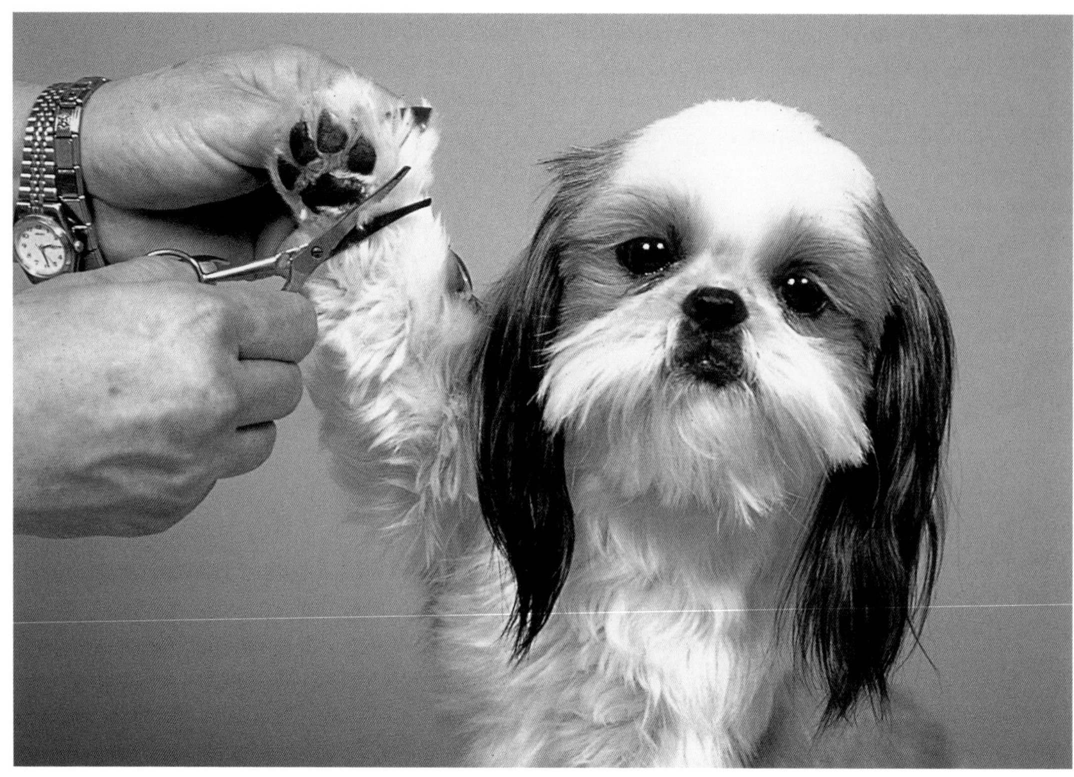

Carefully cut away the hair that grows around your Shih Tzu's toes to keep the foot clean and mat free.

little bit each week. Over time, the quick inside your dog's nail will retreat, and your Shih Tzu will soon enjoy the comfortable feeling that comes with well-trimmed nails.

If, by chance, you do hit the quick, hold the end of your Shih Tzu's nail against the tip of your finger and the bleeding will stop. You can also get styptic powder to stop bleeding, but usually your Shih Tzu won't need that much help.

All this sounds good in theory, but countless Shih Tzu owners have experienced squirming little dogs who pull their feet away any time the nail trimmer comes near. If your dog is pulling his feet away, take these steps to condition him to accept toenail trimming:

- First, teach your dog to be comfortable having his feet touched without the nail clipper. Hold his paw gently. If he tries to pull his paw away, move your hand with it. (Never pull at his foot—that just creates a tug-of-war with his paw.) If you're persistent, he'll eventually calmly let you hold his foot. Reward him, and tell him he's a star!
- Repeat the exercise every day. After he's comfortable with

his foot being held, rub his paws and massage his feet. Now, he's used to having his feet handled.

- Hold the nail clippers and give him a treat.
- Trim just one nail (and be sure *not to hurt him*) and give him a treat.
- The next day, trim two nails.
- The day after that, trim three nails.
- Build up to a regular routine of trimming all his toenails.

Grooming as a Health Check

When you're done combing your dog, do a quick health check. Do you feel any lumps or bumps? Are there any little scabs or signs of allergies? If you see anything unusual or different, have it checked out by your veterinarian.

How is your dog's weight? Is he a bit too thin, or a bit too chubby?

Don't Forget the Dewclaws

Some Shih Tzu have a little "thumb" located on their ankles. This little toe is called a *dewclaw*. The nails on the dewclaws grow rapidly, because they aren't worn against the ground. Remember to trim the nails on your pooch's dewclaws. If you don't, they can quickly grow long and become embedded in your dog's leg.

Trimming Furry Feet

When you're trimming your Shih Tzu's toenails, look at the bottom of his feet. It's common for the hair between his pads to grow quickly, and this hair can easily mat. Snip away any excess hair with a pair of blunt-nosed scissors.

Also, massage between the pads of his feet and between his toes, looking for any lumps, bumps, mats, or icky creatures, like ticks.

EAR CARE

Underneath all that hair on your dog's head are two ears that need special care. Shih Tzu, like other drop-eared dogs, frequently develop ear infections. With ears that flop down, plus lots of hair around the ear, there just isn't a lot of air circulating in the area. The warm, often moist ear canal is a prime breeding ground for yeast and bacterial infections.

It's important to prevent ear infections before they start. Every time you brush your Shih Tzu, check his ears. Be sure they smell clean and fresh. Watch for accumulating earwax—a sign that your dog might have an ear infection.

You can clean your Shih Tzu's ears with a small cotton ball, but don't use a cotton swab. If you put a cotton swab inside your dog's ear, a movement of his head could cause serious

The large, prominent eyes of the Shih Tzu make them especially prone to problems. Check the eyes regularly to make sure they are clean.

damage. Special ear-cleaning products are available for drop-eared dogs. Your veterinarian or your dog's breeder can recommend products that will work best for your dog.

Shih Tzu have more than their share of ear infections, so make an appointment with your veterinarian if you see an excessive amount of ear wax or smell an unpleasant odor in your dog's ears.

The hair that grows in your Shih Tzu's ears may need to be plucked. Ask your groomer or veterinarian to do this, or to show you how to pluck these hairs as painlessly as possible.

EYE CARE

Shih Tzu are prone to eye problems, so it's important to keep a careful watch on your dog's eyes. Your dog has large, prominent eyes that are targets for all kinds of problems.

You can help your dog by keeping his hair out of his eyes. If he has long hair on his head, put it in a topknot or tie it into a braid (a fun and practical answer for a Shih Tzu). Even if he has a short haircut on his head, stray hairs can get in his eyes. Pay attention to his eyes to make sure they are free of fur.

If he looks like he's in any pain—rubbing his eyes, "scrubbing" his face against objects, or squinting—look to see if there's a hair in his eyes.

Occasionally, Shih Tzu can have serious eye injuries and

won't feel the pain. Even if your dog isn't showing obvious signs of pain, check his eyes regularly.

Grooming Safety

Never leave your Shih Tzu unattended for a single second in the sink, on a counter top, or on a table. If you realize you forgot something you need, pick up your wet dog and carry him with you while you find it.

DENTAL CARE

Little dogs have big dental problems, and Shih Tzu have more problems than most. Your Shih Tzu has the same number of teeth as a German Shepherd, and they all have to fit in that little, short face. Dogs with shortened muzzles, such as Shih Tzu, Pugs, and Pekingese, don't have the same alignment of their teeth as a long-nosed dog. The natural cleaning action caused by the friction between the teeth of longer-muzzled dogs happens less for your dog.

Your Shih Tzu's breath shouldn't smell like, well—dog breath. Bacteria are the cause of bad breath. Those nasty bugs don't just stay in your dog's mouth—they circulate around his body, affecting his kidneys, heart, and liver. Dental disease will shorten your dog's life. Bad breath can also be a symptom of several diseases, including serious kidney and liver problems.

If your dog's breath smells unpleasant, or if you notice a change of odor of any kind, make an appointment with your veterinarian.

Every Shih Tzu should have his teeth brushed daily. At the very least, brush them twice a week. (Although you wouldn't be too happy if your teeth were only brushed twice a week, would you?) Don't use human toothpaste—that will upset your Shih Tzu's tummy. You can find toothpaste formulated especially for dogs at your veterinarian's office. Dogs don't generally want flavors like mint or vanilla—so their toothpaste comes in flavors like beef and poultry.

Most doggy toothbrushes are designed to work for a Labrador or a Golden Retriever, but you can find plenty of products scaled to your dog's small mouth. Try a cat toothbrush, apply the toothpaste to a square of gauze, or purchase a small rubber brush that attaches to your finger. Experiment to see what feels most comfortable to you and your dog.

Remember to clean clear into the back molars—they're the teeth that need it most. Dogs can't floss, so encourage your dog to do the next best thing: chew on safe toys. Some Shih Tzu aren't enthusiastic about toys, but look for toys your dog enjoys.

Ask a Well-Coifed Shih Tzu

If you see a beautifully groomed Shih Tzu, ask his owner where she goes for grooming. The owner will be flattered, and you might find a great groomer.

Throw the toy, play tug-of-war, or encourage him to squeak the squeaker inside. These toys can act much like dental floss and reduce the buildup of plaque.

Even when you brush diligently, your Shih Tzu must have professional cleanings occasionally. Your veterinarian will put your dog under anesthesia and carefully clean his teeth and get all the plaque from around his gum line. How quickly your dog accumulates tartar and needs his teeth cleaned depends on many things, including how often you brush his teeth, how much he chews toys, and his genetics. Some dogs need teeth cleaning every 6 months, while others may be able to go a couple of years between cleanings.

PROFESSIONAL GROOMERS

Shih Tzu are one of the breeds that keep groomers busy. Most likely, your dog will be going to the groomer about once a month. It's essential that you find someone who is kind and gentle with your dog—not to mention has the skills to keep your dog looking his best.

In most states, human hairdressers must pass a test to show they're knowledgeable in their work. There aren't any such requirements for dog groomers. While some have pursued extensive training, many are entirely self-taught, so the abilities and professionalism of groomers varies widely.

A professional groomer can keep your Shih Tzu looking and feeling his best.

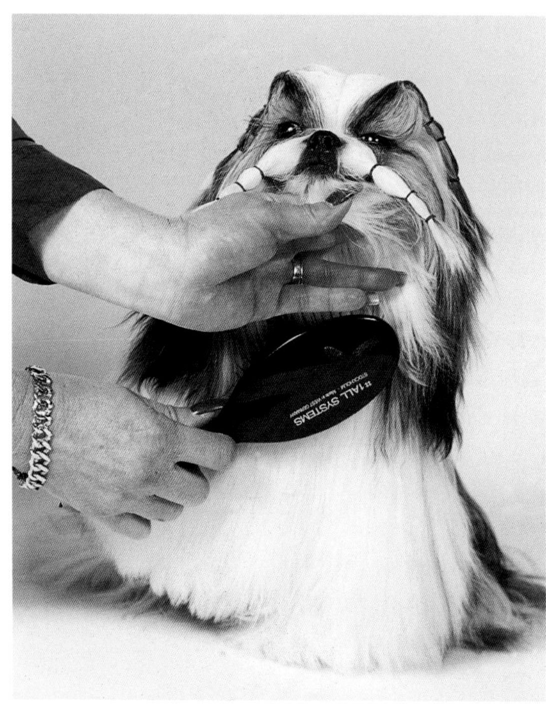

To find a competent, kind groomer, ask your breeder or your veterinarian for recommendations. Some veterinarians even have groomers working in their practices.

Some of the best in the profession have undergone extensive training and testing to obtain the Certified Professional Groomer designation from International Professional Groomers, Inc. This is a tough test, which requires passing written exams and grooming dogs under the scrutiny of demanding judges. The Certified Professional

Getting the best look for your Shih Tzu may require using a professional groomer with years of experience in the breed.

Groomer designation certainly shows a commitment to providing excellent service to you and your dog.

No matter where you get your recommendation—and no matter how qualified the groomer seems on paper—always go for a visit and decide for yourself. See if the shop is clean and whether the groomer is gentle. See what sort of rapport she has with the dogs she grooms.

The younger your puppy is when you start taking him to the groomer, the better. This is an important part of his life, and if he learns to accept it as a puppy, he'll be calmer and happier throughout his lifetime of grooming visits.

One of the most important commitments you can make to your Shih Tzu is to keep him well groomed. If you don't, life will be unpleasant and uncomfortable for him. When you do keep him well groomed, he will enjoy a wonderful lifetime with you. Doesn't he deserve the best?

Chapter 6

TRAINING AND BEHAVIOR of Your Shih Tzu

When people think of a snap-to obedience dog, the word Shih Tzu probably doesn't leap to mind. But, don't be too quick to discount your little dog's abilities. While it's true your Shih Tzu will never herd sheep like a Border Collie or retrieve a bird like a Golden Retriever, you'll find he's a smart and loving companion. He'll readily learn all kinds of useful commands (and some that are just fun) if you give him the chance.

If you've ever trained a dog with old-fashioned choke chains and military-style commands, you'll find that they don't work on a Shih Tzu. Your sweet, adorable, friendly dog will dig his little paws into the ground and refuse to learn a thing. No mere human ever won a war of wills with a determined Shih Tzu.

Happily, you don't need to have a battle of wills to train your Shih Tzu. Today's modern methods emphasize food, fun, and love—all of your dog's very favorite things!

This chapter covers socialization, housetraining, and basic manners—everything your dog needs to thrive in the human world he lives in.

POSITIVE TRAINING METHODS

Two types of positive training techniques are used: *clicker training* and *lure and reward training*.

Clicker Training

Clicker training uses a clicker, which is a little, hand-held, low-tech device with a metal strip that makes a sharp, distinctive *click* when you push it. Dogs learn to recognize that the *click* is a magically good thing when it is paired with a food reward. *Click*, treat. *Click*, treat. Within minutes, every dog loves to hear the *click*.

After the dog understands that a *click* means good things, the clicker is used to highlight good behavior. The instant the dog does something you like, you *click* the behavior. Think of a camera click—that clicking sound captures a moment in time. Clicker training captures a dog doing something right and rewards the dog with a *click*, and then a treat.

When Repetition Is too Much of a Good Thing

Shih Tzu aren't Border Collies. They don't like to repeat things over and over and over and over. When training your Shih Tzu, make it a rule to only practice a command two or three times. After that, your independent little Shih Tzu is likely to look at you and think "I choose not to do this again—not even for a cookie."

Lure and Reward Training

Lure and reward training is equally positive. In this method, a lure (such as a yummy treat) helps the dog find the position you want. For example, if you want your dog to sit, you move the treat over his head, and he follows the treat with his nose until he automatically sits. You've lured him into place with the treat, and you'll reward him with the treat when he does what you want him to do.

This chapter uses a lure and reward system of training—but don't worry. If you like clicker training, just click when the instructions tell you to say "Good!"

SOCIALIZING YOUR SHIH TZU

Shih Tzu were born to be lovers. They are devoted to their human families and have the attitude that strangers are just friends they haven't met yet.

Even though this is a naturally social breed, if you don't do your part to help your puppy, he won't enjoy the happy and exuberant embrace of life that he should. If you expose him to new people and places when he's young, he's likely to enjoy humans, other dogs, and travel throughout his long life. If you fail to do this, he'll be a more worried, less friendly dog. He might even be on his way to becoming one of the small minority of Shih Tzu who are aggressive.

All puppies, including yours, need socialization to learn how to respond to people, new places, and other dogs. For the happiness and safety of your little buddy, you must expect to intensely socialize your Shih Tzu puppy.

The First 12 Weeks

The first 12 weeks of a Shih Tzu's life have a big impact on everything that follows. Because these weeks are spent at the breeder's home, it is vital that you purchase your Shih Tzu from someone who is dedicated to the breed and who socializes her puppies.

During these formative weeks, a puppy learns about dog behavior. When he plays with his littermates, he learns to be gentle in play. From his mother and siblings, he learns about canine social hierarchies and where he belongs in them.

If you take a Shih Tzu puppy away from his mother and

littermates too soon, he most likely will never learn to enjoy the company of other dogs.

Your puppy must learn other lessons during this time. He should be walking on different surfaces so that he doesn't fear new sensations, and he should meet gentle children and adults in the safety of his home. Don't consider purchasing a Shih Tzu from anyone who doesn't give this early education to your prospective puppy. Many studies have proven that dogs who get this early exposure grow up to be healthier, more confident, and smarter than puppies who don't.

But the love and attention of the breeder is just the beginning. You need to take your dog to the next level after he's settled into your home.

Training Treats

Shih Tzu have a tendency to become chubby, so be careful with training treats. Use tiny amounts. A piece the size of a pencil eraser is plenty! If your dog is on a diet, choose healthier, low-fat treats. Even tiny pieces of carrots make good treats.

Three Months to Six Months

The more good experiences your puppy has with people, the more confident and happy he will be for his entire life. For the first few days after you bring your new puppy home, keep him at home with you and let him bond with you. Then, it's time to explore the world together!

Your goal should be for your dog to meet 100 kind, friendly, gentle people in 100 days. Go to pet stores, coffee shops, the vet's office (without getting shots), and home supply stores. Take your puppy to meet the groomer, and let him play with the nice kids down the street.

Exposing your Shih Tzu puppy to different people and environments in a positive way helps him grow to be a confident, friendly, and outgoing dog.

Good Experiences Help

Remember that socialization should involve only good experiences! If a not-so-nice child pulls your puppy's ears or tail, it will teach him to fear children. If a not-so-tuned-in adult picks him up by his ribcage and it hurts, he won't want to be picked up by strangers.

Supervise your puppy's socialization, and make sure he's having fun.

If your puppy shows signs of stress, like tucking his tail under his rump, putting his ears down, holding his head down, or yawning, slow down. Take a few steps back. Gradually move closer to the source of stress once your Shih Tzu begins to accept the new experience.

Socialization is important, but so is your puppy's health. Until he has completed his vaccinations for parvo and distemper, don't let him walk on grass in public parks, rest stops, or other places that unimmunized dogs may have pottied. Carry your puppy in your arms instead.

When you go places where you know only well-cared-for dogs hang out (such as a responsible friend's home), put your puppy on the ground and let him explore!

Puppy kindergarten is great for Shih Tzu at this age—it's a place where your dog can learn to interact appropriately with humans and other dogs. Always check out the class before signing up, however. Do not take your dog to a kindergarten that allows big puppies to pounce on little ones or allows one dog to bully another! That will teach your dog to be afraid of other dogs.

Six Months and Older

You didn't stop having new experiences after kindergarten, and neither should your dog. Keep building on the great beginning you and your breeder have given your dog.

Take obedience classes that use positive training methods. When your puppy is over a year old, think about taking an agility class. Consider preparing him for the Shih Tzu specialty: animal-assisted therapy.

Your little dog has too much to offer the world—and too much curiosity—to spend all his time at home. Some people think they're protecting their small dogs by always leaving them at home, but they really make life harder for their little buddies. Trips to the vet and the groomer become increasingly frightening experiences for these unsocialized dogs. The best ticket to a happy life is to get out and enjoy it! Let your great little dog see the wonders of the world around him. You will have a great time exploring things together and making new friends for both of you, everywhere you go.

HOUSETRAINING YOUR SHIH TZU

The best ticket to a happy life is to get out together and enjoy it!

Shih Tzu have a wonderful reputation for many things. They're considered among the sweetest, easiest to live with dogs on the planet. They have a reputation for being almost magical in understanding human moods and needs.

They do have one minor flaw in their reputation, though. They are known as one of the most difficult breeds to housetrain. Although some Shih Tzu catch on to the idea quickly, others will look lovingly at you, wag their tails, and potty in the house. Most toy breeds can be difficult to housetrain, but Shih Tzu are one of the most difficult of the toy breeds.

Still, with gentle persistence, your dog can be housetrained. It might be more of a challenge than it is for most breeds, but you and your dog can do this.

Why Is Housetraining Such a Challenge?

Some Shih Tzu do catch on to housetraining quickly. They are the exception. This doesn't have anything to do with the intelligence of your dog—most Shih Tzu simply don't understand the concept as quickly as most other dogs.

No one knows why it's harder to housetrain Shih Tzu, but there may be a genetic factor involved. Other short-faced Asian breeds, including Pugs and Pekingese, are also hard to housetrain. Some ancestor 1,000 years ago may have contributed to the problem!

Other small-breed dogs are also generally harder to housetrain than are their larger cousins. Part of the small-dog problem may come from a different sense of space. A toy-sized dog may dutifully trot over to a corner of the room to pee and think he's done the right thing. In his mind, he's gone as far away from his bed as a full-sized dog who's gone to the far end of the yard. The idea of going what seems to be a very long distance away to pee is a tricky one for a lot of smaller dogs.

Like other small-breed dogs, Shih Tzu puppies mature more

Housetraining your Shih Tzu may prove a challenge, but with patience and persistence, it will happen.

slowly during their first few months of life. Your puppy may be 6 months or older before he really has control of his digestive functions in any meaningful way. Expect to continue to work on the fundamentals of housetraining well into your puppy's adolescence.

Part of the problem may also be the way that toy dog puppies are raised—even by the best breeders. Veterinary behaviorists have completed studies that indicate puppies develop a preference for where they potty by the time they're 8.5 weeks old. Large breed puppies are almost always pottying outside by that age (it isn't fun to clean up after a Saint Bernard, even if he's only 6 weeks old). Toy breeders usually keep their puppies inside during those early weeks. Good breeders keep their puppies' areas very clean, but even so, the pups may be pottying on newspaper, bedding, and maybe even carpeting. The lesson is firmly ingrained in your Shih Tzu before he ever comes home: Grass is a weird place to potty. It's even worse for puppy-mill dogs, who may live, play, and potty all in a small, filthy cage.

What to Do

The bottom line: You absolutely can housetrain your Shih Tzu, but most likely it will take a more consistent and patient approach than for most dogs.

This is what you must do to housetrain your Shih Tzu:

Confine Your Dog

A puppy cannot understand the concept of housetraining if you let him roam the whole house—or even an entire room. He must be confined to a space he understands. If you don't keep your puppy confined to a space he can understand and manage, he will never learn to be reliably housetrained.

Keep an eye on him all the time. If you can't keep an eye on him, put him in his crate or an exercise pen, where he's likely to let you know if he needs to potty. If you want to keep your hands free, tie a 6-foot leash to your waist, so he's hanging out with you but can't run over to the corner for a potty break. (This also teaches him to follow you—a great lesson for your puppy.)

When you leave the house, confine your puppy to his crate or an exercise pen.

Take Your Dog Outside

Remember, your puppy didn't learn to potty on grass from his mom. He has no idea what you expect him to do when you put him out the door. He may feel lonely. He may decide to hunt bugs. It probably won't occur to him to potty. Go out there with him and wait until he potties. When he does, praise him! Have a party! Let him know he's a little puppy genius!

A word for the girls here: A female Labrador Retriever may never notice prickly bits of grass or uncomfortable rocks. A female Shih Tzu probably will. Look for a comfortable spot for her. She might prefer a part of the lawn that doesn't have grass, such as a garden area. In winter, you might have to shovel snow to give her a usable spot.

Housetraining Problems

A couple of difficulties that might seem like housetraining problems actually have different causes. Understanding these issues and dealing with them can help you and your dog enjoy each other better.

Territorial Marking

Male toy dogs are notorious leg-lifters. A male dog can be otherwise perfectly housetrained but still mark his territory. Unfortunately, sometimes that territory is your sofa.

Although many toy breeds are worse than Shih Tzu, this breed still has some

Housetraining an Adult Dog

Chances are, if you've adopted an adult Shih Tzu, he has never learned reliable housetraining habits. With persistence, your adult Shih Tzu can be housetrained. Train your adult dog by following the same steps as with a puppy. Expect him to take a while longer—he has to unlearn his old behavior and adopt new ways of doing things.

Recognize the Signs

Some dogs never go to the door and bark to be let out. Your dog may walk in a circle. He may trot around restlessly. He might just give you a certain look. Pay attention to your dog, and figure out the signs he gives when he needs to potty. When you see those signs, get him outside immediately!

Teach a "Permission to Potty" Command

When your dog potties, say "Good potty!" (or whatever word you choose) and reward him with petting and maybe a treat. Eventually, when you say "Potty!" your dog will potty. When your puppy understands this, you've got it made. You will have a puppy who understands what you want, and housetraining will no longer be a mystery to him. (A permission to potty command not only helps Shih Tzu connect the dots and learn the concept, it's also a great lifetime command. Just think how helpful it will be to tell your dog to go potty before you go for a car ride, or when you're traveling and have to take him to unfamiliar places.)

Be Persistent

You will do everything right—and your puppy may still be completely mystified about what you're asking for months. Don't give up. Keep him appropriately confined when you can't supervise him. Keep having a party when he potties outside. Keep doing what you're supposed to. One day, the light of recognition will dawn on his little face, and all the effort will have been worth it.

Getting your dog outside often enough is necessary for successful housetraining.

boys who think marking territory is a good way to pass the time. The problem is worse in households with multiple unneutered, male, toy-sized dogs.

Neutering your dog, especially when he's a puppy, is the best defense against territorial leg-lifting.

If you have a marker, consider using a belly band (also called a cummerbund). This is a strip of cloth with an absorbent pad that goes around the dog's tummy to manage the problem. It's not a perfect solution, but it sure beats constantly cleaning the sofa.

Submissive Urination

Does your dog urinate when you greet him, pet him, or when he's excited? He's probably trying to tell you that he's no challenge to you. Peeing at those times is doggy terms for, "I'm no threat. You're in charge!"

Don't respond to submissive urination by yelling at your Shih Tzu or punishing him in any way. Because he is urinating to show that he's submissive to you, he will only pee more if he thinks you're angry.

Your dog will eventually grow out of this problem—if you

help him. Greet the dog with your hand under his chin, rather than over his head. The scariest greeting for any dog is for a hand to come over his head or back—the threat of this greeting is multiplied when the dog is the size of a Shih Tzu.

Be very matter-of-fact when you come and go. When you're all excited about coming and going, the dog thinks something major is happening. A worried dog is a peeing dog. Place a washable mat at the front door, so if your dog does "leak" as he greets you, it's not a big deal. Just wash the mat.

Indoor Toilet Systems for Small Dogs

Lots of Shih Tzu live in high-rises. After all, this breed makes a great apartment dog—quiet and small. Also, lots of Shih Tzu owners work all day and know better than to leave a small, friendly dog in the yard for the first dognapper to grab.

For Shih Tzu who don't have easy access to the yard, an indoor toilet system is a great idea. Here are some ideas that work for Shih Tzu and their owners:

Many small-dog owners prefer to train them to have a designated potty spot inside.

Stool Eating

Some puppies are stool eaters. People used to believe that dogs who ate their feces had some sort of nutritional deficiency, but that is rarely true. No one really knows why dogs eat poop, although some puppies may be imitating their mothers, who naturally clean up after puppies. Fortunately, it's usually a harmless, although gross (to humans), habit.

To end the habit, go outside with your puppy. As soon as he defecates, praise him and call him over to you to give him a treat. With your direction, most puppies outgrow this habit by the time they're about 6 months old.

Housetraining Pads

Available at pet supply stores, housetraining pads have been treated with an odor that humans don't smell but that smells like urine to a dog. These pads have absorbent material on one side and plastic backing on the other, so you can safely place them on most floors without damaging your home. Because of the attractive (to a dog) odor, Shih Tzu will understand what you want and potty right on the pad.

Litter Boxes

For generations, cats have used litter boxes in the house. Finally, some people have realized that the same concept works for small dogs.

Use a large-sized cat litter box (or a large, short-sided plastic box of any kind). You can lots of different materials as litter. You can buy dog litter. You can also experiment with cat litter, but be sure *not* to use clumping litter. (If your dog swallows clumping litter, it forms into a solid mass in his tummy and might require emergency surgery if it gets caught in his digestive system.) If you have a cat, don't be tempted to let the dog and cat share a litter box. It's a weird fact of life that dogs like the taste of cat waste (yuck!). Even worse, your cat probably won't use the litter box if your dog is using it—and then you have a cat housetraining disaster on your hands.

Grass Boxes

You can bring a yard (of sorts) inside for your dog. Think of it as a mini-lawn in your home (or on your balcony) for your mini-dog.

Build a box, fill it with dirt, and put sod on top. The sod must be replaced every few weeks, unless you have a green thumb.

Teaching Your Dog To Use His Indoor System

Just because you've developed a great indoor toilet system for your dog doesn't mean he'll know he's supposed to use it. You have to train your dog to potty in the correct place indoors, just as you train a dog to go outdoors.

Because housetraining pads are treated with an attractive (to a dog) odor, your dog will have a clue that it's okay to potty on that spot. But to encourage your dog to potty in his litter box or

Selecting the right type and size of crate—and using it correctly—assists in the housetraining process.

grass box, place a little of his waste on the spot.

Watch your dog for signs that he needs to potty (just as you would if you were going to take him outdoors). When he lets you know it's time, take him over to his box or pad. Train him to obey the permission to potty command the same way you would if he were pottying outside.

One of the advantages of an indoor system is that you can leave your dog confined in a room (or an exercise pen) with his box or pads. If he needs to potty in your absence, he's already been introduced to the system, and he's likely to use it when the need arises. You'll both be more comfortable knowing he has that option!

CRATE TRAINING YOUR SHIH TZU

When new Shih Tzu owners look at a crate, they almost all have the same thought: They'd *never* leave their sweet little dog in a cage. It looks like doggy prison.

Don't look at a crate through human eyes. Look at it through Shih Tzu eyes. Your Shih Tzu sees his crate as a place of his very own, where he's safe and secure no matter what else is going on. He'll love having digs of his very own.

Crate Size

Like Goldilocks, your Shih Tzu's crate shouldn't be too big or

Housetraining Difficulties

If your Shih Tzu is usually very good with his housetraining but suddenly starts having accidents, it's time to call your veterinarian.

Urinary tract infections can make it impossible for a dog to control his urge to urinate. Other health problems, including diabetes and kidney problems, can cause housetraining woes.

If he whimpers or cries when he potties, or if he tries to potty and can't—take him to the veterinarian immediately. These are symptoms of what might be a medical emergency.

too small—it needs to be just the right size. It should be large enough for him to stand in and turn around—if it's too small, it isn't comfortable. On the other hand, especially when you're using it as part of a housetraining regimen, you don't want the crate to be too big. If it would comfortably accommodate a Great Dane, your Shih Tzu will probably use one corner as a toilet—not the concept of housetraining!

Your dog's crate should be just as comfy as any bedroom. Make sure it has a nice, thick pad for snuggling on. (If he tends to chew dog beds, line the crate with towels instead.) He should have chew toys in his crate to pass the time.

This comfy, cozy little room certainly isn't doggy prison!

How to Crate Train

The most important thing you can do is to make your Shih Tzu associate his crate with all things pleasant and fun. Of course, that usually means food to a Shih Tzu.

Put a treat in the crate and encourage your pup to go into the crate to get it. When you ask your dog to go into his crate, use a consistent command, such as "Crate" or "Go kennel." A reward should always follow for going into the crate.

After your Shih Tzu has learned to happily trot into his crate, briefly close the door while he's chewing his treat. The next time he goes into the crate, close the door for a few minutes. Feed your dog his meals in his crate. Build up the amount of time he spends in his crate, so he's happy and comfortable in it when you leave the house and when he sleeps at night.

Just because your dog is in a crate doesn't mean he's not part of the family. Keep the crate in a busy part of the house, such as in the living room or the bedroom.

The Crate Should Be a Fun Place!

Never, ever use your dog's crate as punishment! If your Shih Tzu does something naughty, and you put him in his crate to punish him, he will think he's being punished every time you put him in his crate. You go to work—and he's punished. You leave the house—and he's punished. It won't take long for your little guy to hate his crate.

So what do you do when he's driving you nuts? It's okay to put him in a crate with a toy if you need some quiet time. But no anger, no yelling, no "You're grounded!" Just quietly put him in the crate for a little rest.

Leadership

Real leaders aren't violent. They don't yell, hit, or threaten. They show, through calm actions and cues that dogs understand, that they are benevolent leaders. Dogs with gentle human leaders in the household are more secure, happier, and more obedient.

How Much Is too Much Crate Time?

Crates are great tools, but don't leave your little buddy in his crate for hours on end. Kids don't live in their bedrooms all day long, and dogs shouldn't live in their crates for more than a couple hours at a time.

How much crate time is too much depends on your dog and what other things happen to him during the day. If he gets plenty of fun, exercise, and interaction with you before and after being in his crate, then he can comfortably hang out in the confined space for longer than if he's just stuck in there because you're busy.

If he's normally in a crate while you're at work, be sure that you or a pet sitter come and let him out during the day. He'll need a walk or play session. If you need to leave him alone while you're at a full day of work, think of a larger confinement area—maybe an exercise pen or a small room (such as a bathroom) with a litter box or housetraining pads in it.

If he has any housetraining accidents in his crate, this is a serious sign he has been in the crate too long. If your dog gets in the habit of soiling his crate, he will learn to hate his crate. It will also be extraordinarily hard to make progress on housetraining once a dog gets in the habit of pottying in his crate.

CANINE LEADERSHIP

Shih Tzu have an independent streak. If you aren't clearly in charge, they'll happily march to their own tune. If your little guy becomes too independent, he won't come when he's called, he won't do well with his grooming, and he'll feel less bonded to you.

A lot of people think Shih Tzu don't need human leaders. After all, your dog certainly isn't going to be a crazed maniac, endangering humans or other dogs. Who cares who's in charge?

Your dog cares. Dogs who run the show aren't happy dogs. In fact, they worry all the time.

Think of the world from your little dog's perspective. Should the strange human be allowed in the house? Should he let the veterinarian give him that injection? Is it okay for that person to

Even small, independent-minded dogs like Shih Tzu need you to help them learn appropriate behavior.

hug his "mom"? If he has to make these decisions, he will make the wrong ones.

If you don't act like a leader, he can't find out the information he needs from you. Worse yet, he thinks you don't know how to take care of him. He doesn't believe he can count on you.

If don't provide leadership, your Shih Tzu will think he has to be the leader. He's likely to become a territorial tyrant and may turn into a nipper. But no matter what your dog does, he'll never feel truly safe and secure. He'll know there's something wrong when the little dog is running the house and the full-sized humans are incompetent (from your dog's perspective).

It's even worse for shy dogs, who can experience round-the-clock panic if they don't think there's a strong leader in the house to protect them.

Follow these guidelines for gentle leadership, and the results will be almost magical. Your dog will be happier, and both of you will feel more bonded. This may be the best gift you can give your little guy.

Give Your Dog Regular Meals

In the world of dogs, the one who controls the food is the leader of the pack. When you put your Shih Tzu's food on the floor and leave it there, you've just told him that he runs the house. Physically give your dog two meals a day (three or four during puppyhood). Put the food down and pick the bowl up when he's done. If he hasn't eaten his meal in about 20 minutes, pick up the bowl with the food in it. Do this, and your Shih Tzu will see you as the Chief Dog.

This simple bit of advice can do more to change your Shih Tzu's behavior than any other single thing you can do. It's so simple, yet every single Shih Tzu on earth will respond to it. For many dogs, it transforms a relationship. Your dog can relax and let you run the house.

Require Your Dog to Earn His Food

Your dog should sit, lie down, or do a trick before you give him a morsel. What does this do? It reminds him that you're in charge. You ask him to do something, and then he gets fed.

If you're worried this will make him sad, you'll find the opposite is true. Dogs who get to work for their dinners are happy—even proud—of their little accomplishments. Your dog is pleasing you and using his brain.

Feeding and Behavior

Feeding your Shih Tzu meals instead of free-feeding him will improve his behavior—and it's good for his health, too. You'll notice if he's skipping his food, which can be the first sign of illness. It gives you control over his weight. Every dog should be fed regular meals, unless a veterinarian has a specific reason for recommending free-feeding a dog.

Decide When Your Dog Is Allowed on the Bed

The top dog doesn't just control the food. The top dog also decides when and where everyone sleeps. When you control where your dog sleeps, again, you're subtly telling him in doggy terms that you run the place. It's fine for your Shih Tzu to sleep in bed with you, if that's what you want. But make it clear that you're making that decision. Teach him "on" and "off" the bed. Play games in which he comes up and down from the bed.

If your dog growls at you in bed, don't let him sleep in bed with you. Have a comfy crate next to the bed, and let him snuggle there for the night. When he growls at you in bed, he's either worried you will hurt him (no fun for him) or telling you that it's his bed and he doesn't want you to move (no fun for you).

Make Your Dog Wait at Doorways

The Chief Dog (remember, that's you!) leads the other dogs places and decides who goes where and when. When you tell your dog to wait while you walk through a door, you're really telling your Shih Tzu that you are in charge.

These exercises don't add a minute to the time you spend with your dog every day. They don't take any special equipment, and they don't require any special training. If you: 1) give your dog regular meals, 2) have him sit (or do another trick) when you feed him or give him attention, 3) decide when and where he sleeps, and 4) tell him to wait at doors, you'll have a calmer, more tractable dog who will be a nicer, happier dog to live with.

If you're a gentle, loving, kind leader, your little guy can relax and follow you everywhere. You will both be able to enjoy each other more.

When you reward your dog for looking into your eyes, you not only enhance your relationship, but you make other kinds of training easier.

PRELIMINARY TRAINING

You can teach your new Shih Tzu a few simple things that will make your life incomparably easier together. Luckily, these behaviors are simple and fun to teach!

Watch Me

The first thing to teach your Shih Tzu is to look adoringly into your eyes whenever you ask him to.

This command could save your little guy's life. A dog who is looking at you can't pay attention to anything else. He can't stare at the cat across the street, and he can't make eye contact with another dog.

Even if your Shih Tzu generally pays attention to you, teaching him to look at you on command will make training every other command much easier. You know how much easier it is to teach children (or adults) something when they're looking at you. The same is true for a dog.

Teaching Watch Me

To teach Watch Me, hold a treat between your eyes and say "Watch me." Your Shih Tzu will stare longingly at the treat. That's the start—he's focusing in your direction.

The *instant* he looks at the treat, say "Good watch me!" (or click your clicker) and reward the dog with the treat.

After the dog is looking at you consistently, hold the treat in your hand (out of sight of the dog). Say "Watch me." If he looks at you, say "Good watch me!" (or click your clicker) and reward him. If he looks at your hand, say "Uh-uh, watch me." If he looks at your face, reward him. If he doesn't understand, then hold the treat in front of your eyes again and remind him of what you want.

Over time, mix up holding treats in front of your eyes and having a treat in your hand until you eventually always have the treat in your hand.

Gradually require your Shih Tzu to look at you for longer periods of time before giving the reward.

Catch

Your Shih Tzu might also want to learn to play Catch with a treat. Playing Catch rewards your dog for paying attention to you.

Teaching Catch

To teach Catch, hold a treat just above your dog's head and say "Catch!" If the treat drops to the ground, quickly pick it up and try again. The only time your dog gets the treat is when he catches it in mid-air.

Do this several times. Many dogs will be catching mid-air in a matter of minutes. Over time, drop the treat from higher and higher distances—and eventually lob it to your dog like a softball pitch.

This game requires your Shih Tzu to pay attention to you—and that's a good thing!

Note: Not all Shih Tzu are famous for their mouth–eye coordination. Some of them never quite get the timing right. Others seem to be stunned by the fact that food is falling on their heads and never get the idea that they're supposed to catch it. Every dog can learn Watch Me—Catch is a bonus command that's fun for those dogs who get the hang of it.

Training With Treats

If you're hesitant to train a dog with treats, you're not up on the latest research.

Many studies have shown that dogs learn faster and behave more reliably when they receive food rewards for doing things right, rather than punishment when they do things wrong.

If training with treats is more effective, more bonding, and more fun, who would want to go back to the old-fashioned training method of jerking on choke collars?

LEASH TRAINING

Obesity is a huge health concern in Shih Tzu. The best antidote is a regular walking routine. Plus, a Shih Tzu will have a wonderful time going for a walks with you. The trick is to go where you want to go—not where your Shih Tzu dictates. Remember, a walk is supposed to be fun for both of you.

Although some Shih Tzu pull and jump at the end of the leash, many others go "on strike." They sit their firm little rears on the ground and won't move. That takes the fun out of a walk very quickly.

Believe it or not, in a couple of days, you and your Shih Tzu can walk together joyfully.

Introducing Your Shih Tzu to a Collar and Leash

Pick a collar or harness that fits your dog. A collar shouldn't be too big, and it should be made of comfortable fabric or leather.

You should be able to put one or two fingers under the collar. If it's too tight, it will be very uncomfortable for your little guy. If it's too loose, he's likely to slip out of it—and that can be life-threatening.

Watch your puppy carefully when he first starts wearing his collar. It must feel very strange to your little guy to have this thing around his neck. Some dogs accept it happily right away, but others paw at the collar and shake their heads. If the collar is too loose, your Shih Tzu can quickly end up with a collar stuck in his mouth or get his paw wedged into the collar.

Tell him how absolutely adorable he is in his fancy new collar, and give him a treat and play with him. As long as the collar is properly fitted, it won't take long for him to get used to having something around his neck.

Your Shih Tzu's collar and leash should fit comfortably, and wearing them should be a pleasant experience.

If you decide to use a harness rather than a collar, use the same procedure as for a collar. In either case, your Shih Tzu should become quickly accustomed to wearing something on his body.

The First Leash Experience

Before you put your dog on a leash, be sure he is comfortable and relaxed wearing his collar or harness.

When he's adjusted to wearing the collar, it's time to teach him the joys of walking on a leash.

Start out in your house and yard. Don't take him for a walk on the leash until he's accustomed to you leading him.

For the first day or two of leash training, let your Shih Tzu lead you. Give him treats and tell him he's a puppy genius—make life fun for him when he's wearing a leash. Wherever he walks, you follow. If he just wants to stand still, that's okay, too. Give him a treat and tell him he's great.

As soon as he's relaxed and comfortable leading you, it's time for you to lead him. Show him a treat, and have him take a few steps with you. Then let him lead you. Then show him a treat

Make the first few days of leash training easy and fun.

and have him walk next to you again.

Soon, he'll love seeing his leash. That will be your ticket to a lifetime of happy walks together. Take the first steps gently and slowly, so that your dog thinks the leash is a great invention and part of your bond.

Give It a Word

Life is always easier for your dog when you give him a word to tell him what's happening. When you're putting his collar on, say a word like "Collar" or be cute and say "Get dressed!" Your smart little Shih Tzu will quickly learn to hold still and put his neck out to make it easier to put on or remove his collar.

Teaching Your Shih Tzu to Walk on a Leash

The point of a walk is for the human to decide which way to go and the Shih Tzu to trot happily alongside. While many Shih Tzu seem to be born to walk happily at the end of a leash, others aren't so easy. Teaching your Shih Tzu to walk calmly on a loose leash will be a gift for both of you.

Happily, you can teach your dog to do this faster than you might think.

Teaching Let's Go!

Your dog should be on a comfortable buckle or snap collar (not a choke collar), and you should have a lightweight 4-foot or 6-foot (1.2- or 1.8-m) leash (not a flexible leash). At first, practice someplace with low distractions, such as your living room or back yard.

Say "Let's go," and start walking. If he pulls, turn in the other direction and say "Let's go!" the instant his leash tightens.

While training your dog to walk nicely on a leash, tell him what a wonderful fellow he is when he trots along nicely beside you.

If he runs out and pulls in the new direction, turn and go a different way, saying "Let's go!"

The moment he's walking on a loose leash, give him a treat and tell him he's a very, very good dog. Very quickly, your dog will figure out that he will never, ever get where he wants to go if he pulls. On the other hand, he'll learn that keeping an eye on you is incredibly fun. Soon, he will be merrily walking on a loose leash!

Once you've really mastered Let's go! in a place with low distractions, practice it somewhere with more noises, smells, and activities. Even if you feel silly, repeat the same procedure. If you consistently and adamantly follow this procedure, your dog will be walking nicely with you within a week.

BASIC TRAINING

Shih Tzu are usually very compliant little dogs. They try to do their best to please you. It's easy for owners to overlook the importance—and the joy—of training these little guys.

Basic training gives your dog a clue as to what you want him to do. It helps him understand that words have meaning. It helps him understand the world of humans, so he can thrive in that world.

Training is also important for your dog's safety. Shih Tzu can be quite independent little guys. If they don't come when they're called or know it's important to sit and stay when asked, they can end up dashing through a door, getting hit by a car, or being injured by a big dog.

Plus, keep in mind that teaching your Shih Tzu is just plain fun.

Sit

Does your dog always do Watch Me on command? If so, it will make learning to sit infinitely easier.

Teaching Sit

To teach the Sit command, hold a treat in front of your Shih Tzu's nose. Slowly pull the treat over the dog's head, between the dog's ears. Almost all dogs will naturally rock back into a sit.

Say "Good sit!" and give the reward *while the dog is in the sitting position.*

If your Shih Tzu doesn't automatically sit, *gently* tuck your finger under his rear to help him into a sit position.

Be Gentle!

If you learned about dog training 30 years ago (or even from some not-so-current trainers today), you were taught to teach a dog to walk with you by jerking on the leash. This is a bad idea for any dog, and it's a terrible idea for your little Shih Tzu. That jerking motion can damage your little dog's neck. It certainly makes training a scary experience for your little buddy. When you turn directions, warn your dog by saying "Let's go!" and showing him a treat or patting your lower leg. Remember that walking together is supposed to be fun!

A happy dog is one who gladly listens to you and tries to please you.

Teaching your Shih Tzu to sit using the lure and reward method is fast, easy, and enjoyable for both of you.

If your dog keeps trying to turn around, you might want to practice in a confined space. Put him on a comfortable chair where he feels safe. He'll back up to the back of the chair, and then you can lure him into a sit.

If you notice that your dog is doing a "sit up and beg" position, you're holding the treat too high. Hold it just above his nose.

Every Shih Tzu, old or young, rescue dog or the puppy of champions, can learn to sit in a few minutes. Don't overlook the magic of this moment. Your dog has just understood what you asked him to do! He did it! You have truly communicated with a creature of another species—and he communicated back. What could be better?

Stay

Be sure your dog knows and understands the Sit command before you start. Sit and Stay are two different commands.

Teaching Stay

After you tell your dog to sit, take a step back about 6 inches (15.2 cm) and gently say "Stay, good sit-stay." *Instantly* and *while he is still sitting*, reward him. He can't learn to sit for 1 minute until he's learned to sit for 1 second.

When he succeeds at a 1-second Sit-Stay, expand the time to 5 seconds, 10 seconds, etc. If he consistently gets up after 15 seconds, for example, give him a 12-second stay and reward him. Help him succeed.

Chain together two or more stays. Tell him to stay and reward him after 10 seconds, then step back and tell him to stay and reward him after another 15 seconds.

Use a happy voice in this exercise. It's hard enough for a small dog to have the courage to sit and stay while you walk away; this exercise really teaches him to have trust and faith in you. Don't yell, "STAY!" Talk in the same happy, relaxed voice you use to train commands like Sit and Let's Go. Stay should be every bit as interesting and enjoyable for your Shih Tzu as shaking hands, rolling over, or jumping for a treat.

When your dog understands Stay, he can pose for photos like this one. What a good dog!

Releasing Your Dog

When is the Stay command over? If you don't tell your dog, he doesn't know. Teach your Shih Tzu a release word. When you say this word, your dog's exercise is finished. He can relax and do whatever he wants to do—or whatever you ask next.

Any word or short phrase will do: "At ease," "You're done," "Off duty," or "Free dog!" Use a word that sticks in your mind. People who herd with their Border Collies say "That'll do," to release their dogs. *Don't* use "good" or other words of praise as your release word! You want to tell your dog he's good in the middle of an exercise—and still have him continue to stay, come, or sit. The release word must be separate and distinct in sound from "good." Also, be careful of words like "okay" that you use a lot in conversation.

Be sure to give your dog his release word at the end of every exercise, so he knows when he's done.

Teaching the Un-Stay

Most people teach their dogs to move—not stay. They give the dog his reward when he's done with the stay—after he's stood up. The dog will do what gets him a reward, so if you reward him for sitting and then getting up—he'll get up instead of stay. Remember: Always give your Shih Tzu the reward when he's doing what you ask him to do!

For your Shih Tzu to want to come whenever you call—even when he's this comfortable—you must make coming to you a very rewarding request.

Come

Shih Tzu are notorious for ignoring their owners when called. They have other things on their minds!

It's important to teach your dog that Come will always be more fun, more joyous, and more entertaining than anything else that could happen in his life that day.

Teaching Come

The Come command must be taught in an enclosed room or a completely fenced-in area. Put your dog on a long leash, but only use it to corral him if he decides to go running in circles. *Don't* pull on the leash when you teach him this fun, energetic, lively command.

It seems counter-intuitive, but the best way to attract your dog to come to you is to position yourself far across the room or yard. If you're close by, you're old hat. When you're across the room, he'll be a bit more anxious to come to you.

Remember, this must be done in a safe, enclosed room or yard—don't take chances with your dog's life by hoping he'll learn to come in an open yard.

For the first few weeks, teaching the Come command is a two-person job. Someone else must hold the dog while you walk away and call the dog. (If you're both in the same household, it's great to call the dog back and forth.) The person holding the dog should be *silent*. You should get the dog revved up and eager to come to you. In a high, happy voice, say "Ready? Ready? Ready?"

Then call him with a very clear, "Come!"

Keep it fun. Use a happy voice. Squat down and clap your hands or turn and run in the other direction. Make yourself interesting and appealing.

When your dog comes to you, treat him and praise him for *at least 15 seconds*. When you come home, your dog doesn't just come up and say "Good," in a monotone. No way! He bounces up and down to tell you he's thrilled, just thrilled to see you. He wiggles, he licks, he snuggles! You need to show the same happiness when your dog comes to you on the Come command. Your dog needs to know that you're excited he came to you—so act like it!

Practice three times a day. Don't over-do this one, because you want to keep this a spontaneous, joyful communication between you and your dog. Doing things over and over and over again is not a Shih Tzu's idea of a good time.

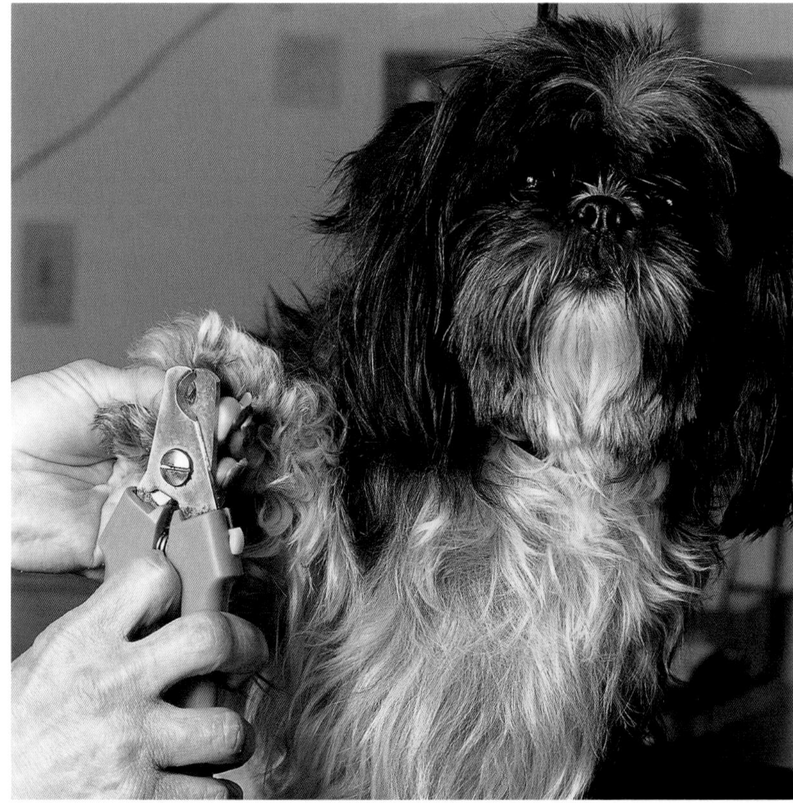

When you need your dog for something somewhat unpleasant, like clipping his nails, don't ask him to come to you—instead, go and get him.

Use a Magic Word for Come

Perhaps you've spent the entire last year saying *"Come!* I said come! This time I really mean it! *Come!* No, stop chasing the cat! I said *come!* This time I really, really mean it! *Come!* No—don't eat the couch! *Come!* This time I really, really, really mean it!" In this case, "come" isn't the best word to use any more. It certainly has no sense of magic to your Shih Tzu.

Use "here" or "front" or something cute and clever. Just don't use a word your dog has been ignoring for years.

What to Do if Your Dog Doesn't Come

Most Shih Tzu will, sooner or later, decide not to come when called. Your dog will meander off and sniff the floor or run around the room madly.

One solution works almost every time, even for the most independent Shih Tzu. Eat his treat. Yes, really. (Obviously, it's a good idea to practice the Come command using a treat that humans like.) Show your dog the treat he could have earned and say "Well, I get the treat."

Pop it in your mouth. Eat the treat like it's the best, most incredible caramel candy you've ever enjoyed. Slurp noisily. Smack your lips. Say just how delicious it is. Don't even think about fake eating the treat. Eat it in front of the dog and swallow it.

He'll get the message loud and clear: He just lost out on the most incredible reward of his lifetime because he didn't come.

Give the dog back to your friend to hold, and show the dog the treat. Once again, call him enthusiastically—and he'll probably come running. If he comes, he gets his treat and tons of praise!

If he's the rare dog who doesn't come after you've eaten his treat, just repeat the process.

Give him back to your friend and call him a third time. He'll come running when he realizes that you really will eat his treats if he doesn't come. When he comes, give him a big "jackpot" of treats. Tell him he's great! Make it incredibly worthwhile for him to come to you!

He will learn it's always more fun to come to you than to ignore you.

Separating Stay from Come

The biggest mistake trainers make at the beginning is to teach the Stay and Come commands together. What could be more natural than saying "Stay," walking across the room, and then calling your dog? The problem is that, from your dog's perspective, it's not natural at all.

If you combine the Stay and Come commands too soon, your dog will have trouble doing a reliable stay for weeks. He'll soon decide that Stay means "sit for a few seconds and then come running."

A reliable Stay can save your Shih Tzu's life some day. Don't jeopardize it by combining the Stay and Come commands too

Teaching Down and then Down-Stay are ways of asking your dog to settle down and calm himself—something you'll both appreciate.

early. It's best to practice both commands separately for at least 3 weeks.

Down

The best way to get your Shih Tzu absolutely under your control and quiet is a Down. If your dog is committed to a Down-Stay, he's not likely to get up. It's the most stable position in dog training, but it's also the most difficult exercise for a small dog to learn. Think about it a little, and it makes a lot of sense. Putting himself in a down position, especially near other dogs, can make your small dog feel extremely vulnerable.

The only way your Shih Tzu can do this exercise successfully is to completely trust you and know that you will keep him safe. That's why your patience and gentleness is especially important in this exercise!

Teaching Down

When teaching the Down command, your dog should be *standing* and relaxed. (Most books and trainers will tell you to teach the Down from a Sit. Dogs who have recently learned to sit and stay are terribly confused when suddenly you tell them

Use Words Consistently

The English language has a countless number of words. Don't confuse your dog by using one word to mean two things! If you use the word "down" to mean "off," use another word or phrase for "lie down." For example, say "lie down," or "drop." You can't have "down" mean "get back on all four feet" and also mean "lie down on the floor."

"Down." If you start with your dog in a standing position, he'll be much less worried when learning this exercise.)

Next, hold a treat between your Shih Tzu's front toes. He'll reach down for the treat and may drop into a down position. Say "Good down!" and give him the treat.

If he doesn't drop, keep the treat on the floor and push it slightly toward his chest. If he physically follows the treat with his nose, his chest will go down on the ground. Say "Good down," and reward him when his chest rests on the ground.

Be patient. Sometimes it takes some maneuvering before your dog learns to down. If he gets frustrated, reward partial success. So, if his chest is on the ground but his rear end is still high in the air, give him a treat and say "Yes!" for the partial success. Build on the partial success until he downs with his whole body—at which time say "Good down," and treat him generously.

Teaching Down on a Chair

Is your Shih Tzu looking at you with those sweet, liquid eyes, clearly not understanding what you're asking? About 90 percent of small dogs learn the Down command with a treat at the toes, but others need a different way to learn it.

A great alternative way to teach the Down command is to teach it on a chair. (This is also easier on your back, and a good alternative if you have trouble bending down to the floor.)

The technique for teaching the Down command on a chair or couch is exactly the same as the traditional technique outlined above, except you hold the treat a few inches below the level of the seat. Your Shih Tzu has to bend his front legs to get to the treat, which means he's well on his way to learning the Down!

Be sure to set the dog up near the edge of the seat, or he won't be able to follow the treat with his nose over the end of the chair.

Also, be sure your dog is comfortable and understands the Down command well on a chair before you try it on the ground. When he does understand it, you should be able to put him on the ground and say "Down," and he'll lie down.

The Down-Stay

Once your dog is comfortable doing a Down, it's time to add the Stay command. Teach this exactly the same way you taught the Sit-Stay.

Your Shih Tzu will be more comfortable and relaxed while grooming if he understands the Down-Stay request.

After you tell your Shih Tzu to down, take a step back about 6 inches (15.2 cm) and gently say "Stay, good down-stay." *Instantly* and *while he is still in the down position,* reward him. Just like the Sit, he can't learn to Down for 1 minute if he hasn't first learned to Down for 1 second.

When he succeeds at a 1-second Down-Stay, expand the time to 5 seconds, 10 seconds, and longer. If he consistently gets up after 15 seconds, for example, give him a 12-second stay and reward him. Help him succeed.

Chain together two or more stays. Tell him to stay and reward him after 10 seconds, then step back and tell him to stay and reward him after another 15 seconds.

Training as a Family Activity

It helps your Shih Tzu if everyone in the household gives him the same rules and the same commands. Your Shih Tzu will bond better with everyone instead of bonding with a single family member.

Agree on what words you'll use. (Does "down" mean "don't jump on people" or does it mean "lie down on the floor"?) Everyone should follow the rules of "Canine Leadership" discussed earlier in this chapter. If you enroll in an obedience class, look for one that welcomes participation from the whole family.

Shih Tzu are clever and will work each family member separately if the family isn't united in how they work with the dog. A 2-year-old child has nothing on the ability of a Shih Tzu to divide and conquer! So, love your dog by being consistent with him.

FINDING A SAFE OBEDIENCE CLASS

A great obedience class is fun for humans and dogs alike. You'll learn new things and meet new people. Your dog will be exposed to new sights and situations in a safe environment.

Before signing up, check out the class. Here are some tips:

Everyone in the family should learn how to train your Shih Tzu.

- **Find a trainer who uses positive, motivational methods.** Training methods that consist of food rewards and fun are best for teaching a Shih Tzu. If the class is an old-fashioned, jerk-and-pull place, go somewhere else. That kind of training isn't effective with an independent breed like the Shih Tzu.
- **Look for a trainer who works with small dogs.** Give her bonus points if she's actually had a small dog of her own. Ask for references from other small-dog owners.
- **Choose a class that matches your style.** Are the people and dogs having fun? Do you relate to the way the trainer teaches? Can your family members participate in class with you?
- **Does the environment feel safe and under control?** Neither you nor your Shih Tzu can relax and learn if big dogs are bouncing at your little guy, even in play.

SHIH TZU PROBLEM BEHAVIORS

Shih Tzu are among the easiest breeds on the planet to live with. These sweet, loving little guys have less behavior problems, as a rule, than do most other breeds. Unlike most small breeds, they tend not to be barkers. They are usually friendly with other dogs and people.

Still, some Shih Tzu have a couple of quirks that may require a little extra time and effort from you. Lots of Shih Tzu see the Come command as entirely elective. They can seem more like cats than dogs when called—they'll take a note and consider it later. But the Come command is too important to let slide.

The other occasional problem is when Shih Tzu become territorial about space, their people, or their toys.

Failing to Come

The Shih Tzu who can hear you blink when he wants your

Shih Tzu can seem to have selective hearing when it comes to responding to certain requests.

Finding A Good Trainer

Take the time to look for a good trainer—don't go for the first trainer listed in the phone book.

Your veterinarian or groomer might be able to suggest someone they respect. If a group does animal-assisted therapy in your community, they may have recommendations—most people doing this type of work are very committed to gentle training.

Also, check out trainers through the Association of Pet Dog Trainers, a national organization that provides ongoing education and certification for dog trainers. This organization emphasizes gentle, nonviolent training methods. Go to www.apdt.com and click on "Trainer Search."

No matter where you get your recommendation, always check out the class yourself! No one knows your dog better than you do.

attention may seem to be deaf when you are calling him. Shih Tzu are devoted and loving little dogs, but they also have an independent streak. It's very important for you to establish a reliable Come command with your little dog!

Review and practice the "Teaching Come" section. Make coming to you a fun and exhilarating exercise for your dog!

Also, work at the canine leadership exercises outlined in this chapter. Be sure to give your Shih Tzu regular meals instead of free-feeding him, and ask him to work (give you a sit, a down, or a trick) for his meals. This gently and joyfully reinforces that you're in charge—and dogs usually come if they think the human really is running the show.

Territorial Aggression

Although most Shih Tzu are friendly, laid-back little guys, a small but noticeable minority can be little tyrants. These are dogs who don't want to share. They don't want to share their toys, their beds, or their personal space—and especially, they don't want to share their people.

If your dog is growling, snapping, or biting people, it's important for you to stop this behavior as soon as it starts.

By taking control of the situation, you can reclaim your spouse, bed, and other valuables, and your dog will be a happier, calmer family member.

When you're the leader, your Shih Tzu respects you.

When Your Dog Won't Let People Near You

Sometimes, a Shih Tzu will decide that his person doesn't belong to anyone else. A person's spouse and friends are all inconveniences at best and enemies at worst. This dog sits like royalty on your lap and growls or snaps when anyone comes near.

Happily, lap guarding is easy to remedy. Take away your lap. If you merely put the dog on the ground when he gets pushy, he won't have a territory to defend. He'll stop growling and calm down.

Meanwhile, let your Shih Tzu know that you like people and want him to as well. The best way for him to decide that other people are a good thing is to have them feed him little treats. Carry treats with you on walks and ask people to feed the dog a little morsel. After he's used to accepting treats on the ground, progress to holding him, and ask a friend to offer the treat.

If your dog is good, he gets the treat. If he growls or snarls, put him back on the floor and have your friend eat the treat. Be sure to use treats that humans like, because it's important for your friend to eat and swallow the treat!

Wait a day or two, and then try again, first treating the dog on the ground and later when he's sitting on your lap. If your friend continues to offer the dog a really yummy treat, sooner or later your Shih Tzu will figure out that it's better to be a good boy than to miss out on such a delicacy.

If your dog reverts to snarling, just say to him, "Oops! Too bad! You've lost your lap privileges!" and put him gently on the floor. That's it—no elaborate discussions, no yelling, and no wailing.

Your Shih Tzu will learn that good behavior allows him to be on your lap and maybe even earns him a treat. Bad behavior gets him placed on the floor, and all the fun is gone. Over time, he'll make the right choice.

Reclaiming Your Bed

The biggest place of conflict is the bedroom. This is especially tense when one spouse wants the dog on the bed and the other doesn't. If your dog growls at your spouse when he comes into the bedroom, growls when you move in bed, or otherwise makes bedtime a nightmare, you need to make some changes.

If you have a dog who is territorial about your bed, or who has been growling or snapping in any other situation, he shouldn't be allowed to sleep on your bed. A crate with a nice cushion and toys, right next to your bed, is a great alternative to sleeping on your bed. He can spend time in the room with you, and you won't have to deal with conflict when you need to sleep. He may whine for a night or two. Ignore him, and he'll soon love his crate every bit as much as he loved your bed.

If you still want your dog to sleep with you, you must work with your dog. For some people, life isn't as good unless a dog is on the bed with them. If you're one of these people, you can work with your territorial Shih Tzu to improve his bedtime manners.

Be prepared to put your dog in a crate if he growls. Keep the comfy crate set up next to your bed, even if you don't plan to use it every night. When your dog growls, scoop him up and unemotionally put him in the crate. Leave him in the crate for the rest of the night. Over time, he'll learn that a growl puts him in the crate. He can choose to behave, or sleep separately.

Teach your dog "On" and "Off." Your dog must learn that *you* decide when he can go on the bed or other furniture. Tell him, "On," and encourage him to come up on the bed. Tell him he's a good boy! Then say "Off!" and reward him for jumping off. Play the "on" and "off" game regularly to reinforce the fact that you decide—not the dog—when he can go on the bed.

Your Behavior Counts, too

Your dog needs your leadership. If you want him to change how he behaves, you have to be completely consistent in how you respond to his behavior. You can't allow him to misbehave one day, and even laugh at his behavior, and then tell him his behavior is unacceptable the next day.

When he does what you want, always reward him with a treat, praise, or fun. Don't ever reward what you don't want, even by laughing.

Remember, dogs who growl and snap aren't happy. Behave consistently, so that your dog can outgrow his bad habits.

Toy and Food Possession

Most Shih Tzu are happy to share their toys. If you have one who is possessive, you need to teach him to share. Happily, that is usually a simple task, as long as you're consistent.

Teach your dog that it's not in his best interest to be territorial with his toys. It's easiest to deal with this problem when the dog is a puppy, but the same techniques can also be applied to an adult dog.

If you feel that your Shih Tzu is ruling the roost, seek the help of a professional trainer or behaviorist.

Give and Take and Give Toys

Make giving a toy into a game! Give the toy to the dog, then take it, and then immediately give it back. Laugh when you do it. Your dog learns that giving up a toy isn't a big deal, since he can expect it back.

Teach Trade

Give your dog a low-value toy—something that isn't one of his favorites. Then hold a very high-value treat (such as piece of steak) and say "Trade!" Almost always, the dog will be thrilled to trade the low-value toy for the high-value treat. After you've done the trade, you can give the dog his original toy back.

When you play "Trade," always make sure you have something in your hand that the dog prefers to whatever he has in his paws. (If he doesn't want to trade, you can just walk away, or better yet, you can eat his high-value treat in front of him, so he knows that he made the wrong choice by not trading.)

Almost every puppy goes through a "keep away" phase where he steals something—inevitably something that's dangerous for a puppy—and runs through the house, seemingly laughing at you because you're too slow to catch him.

"Trade" is the best response to this not-so-funny game. If your Shih Tzu knows that *Trade* means he'll be getting the yummiest treat in the household, he's likely to swap whatever dangerous thing he's got in his mouth for your first-class treat.

It's important that you *always* give the dog the best deal in the trade—you want him to come to you when he's stolen a bottle of medicine or a broken shard of glass. He won't willingly give up the "toy" if he doesn't think he's going to get something great in exchange.

Over time, your dog will learn that *Trade* is a great game, and that he doesn't need to horde anything.

Seeking Professional Help

Very rarely, a Shih Tzu will have patterns of behavior that are scary. He'll try to bite you, or he'll be so aggressive with other people or other dogs that you don't know what to do. Very rarely, Shih Tzu can develop separation anxiety, which makes them destructive or self-destructive when you are away.

If a problem can't be resolved with training, you may need to consult a veterinary behaviorist. This is a veterinarian with specialized training in canine problem behaviors. This dedicated professional will assess the problem behavior and develop a plan of action to resolve the problem. This may include a program of desensitizing the dog to whatever triggers the behavior. The veterinarian may prescribe medication for your dog, such as anti-anxiety medication, to help keep your dog calm while you work on the behavior change.

To find a veterinary behaviorist, ask your veterinarian for a recommendation. You can also find a listing of veterinary behaviorists at the website of the American College of Veterinary Behaviorists at www.dacvb.net.

Teach Drop It

Drop It is a game similar to *Trade*. When you're playing with your dog, *gently* take a toy from his mouth and say "Good drop it," and then give him a treat. That's the beginning of *Drop It*. He'll learn to give you the toy (or drop it at your feet) to get something better.

Your Shih Tzu already loves you. Train him to understand your language, give him clear direction, and his life will be even more joyful. He will bond with you in ways that you can't yet imagine. Get the leash out and have some fun together!

Chapter 7

ADVANCED TRAINING AND ACTIVITIES

With Your Shih Tzu

Once your Shih Tzu knows basic obedience skills, you can discover a whole world of fabulous activities to share with your well-behaved little dog. The fun has just begun!

This chapter gives you information about a lot of sports and activities, but there's one that every Shih Tzu owner should especially consider: animal-assisted therapy. Therapy dogs visit people in hospitals, nursing homes, schools, and other places where contact with a sweet little dog can bring people joy. Shih Tzu may be the most talented of all breeds at this rewarding, important work.

But therapy isn't the only activity your Shih Tzu might enjoy. Is your little guy fast on his feet? Try agility. Do you love his innate Shih Tzu sense of humor? Teach him some tricks to keep that smart little brain of his thinking.

You're already bonded with your Shih Tzu. Do some activities together, and you'll find a depth of communication and understanding that you might have thought only happened on *Lassie* reruns.

THE AKC CANINE GOOD CITIZEN TEST

If you're thinking about doing animal-assisted therapy with your Shih Tzu, he'll have to pass the Canine Good Citizen (CGC) test. Even if therapy work isn't for you and your dog, you may want to take this test, anyway.

The CGC test evaluates the most important skills any dog can have—walking politely on a loose leash, accepting petting and grooming, and staying under control when there's another dog nearby. Any dog, with some basic obedience training and a little leadership from you, has the ability to pass this test.

Passing the CGC test demonstrates that you have a trained, capable, intelligent dog who is an asset to his community. Fittingly, dogs who pass the test receive an official certificate from the American Kennel Club (AKC) that you can frame and hang in the hallway. When your dog has passed the test, it's proper to put the initials "CGC" after

Accepting petting and grooming is part of the Canine Good Citizen test. Most Shih Tzu can ace that part!

your dog's name—for Canine Good Citizen.

Gaining a CGC for your dog is proof to yourself and others that you and your Shih Tzu accomplished something together. It's something you can be proud of.

To find trainers and testing sites for the CGC, go to the American Kennel Club website at www.akc.org.

Test Requirements

First, the pledge! Before taking the Canine Good Citizen test, you'll be required to sign the Responsible Dog Owners Pledge. It's the kind of pledge every dog owner should happily sign. It says that you'll take care of your dog's health, safety, exercise, and training needs, as well as his quality of life. You'll also agree to show responsibility by doing things such as cleaning up after your dog in public places and never letting your dog infringe on the rights of others. Your Shih Tzu is then tested on the following:

- Accepting a friendly stranger
- Sitting politely for petting
- Appearance and grooming
- Out for a walk (walking on a loose lead)
- Walking through a crowd
- Sit and down on command and staying in place
- Coming when called
- Reaction to another dog
- Reaction to distraction
- Supervised separation

Did You Know?

In some cities, apartment and condominium complexes only accept dogs who pass the Canine Good Citizen test.

ANIMAL-ASSISTED THERAPY

Shih Tzu, possibly more than any other breed of dog, are little love-sponges. Most of them seem to sense just what people need to feel better. If you have a Shih Tzu who loves new people and likes to get out of the house, think about becoming a therapy team. It will be incredibly rewarding for both you and your dog.

Therapy dogs visit people in hospitals, hospices, nursing homes, schools, and libraries. Some dogs help bring a light of recognition to a person with advanced Alzheimer's disease. Others sit quietly next to a child who is trying to improve her reading skills. Others participate in physical therapy sessions with people recovering from injuries.

There is a special need for your sweet little dog in this work. Most therapy dogs are big dogs. Although every dog who performs this work brings something special to the task, your Shih Tzu's ability to sit on beds and laps has a charm that a big dog can't match. Some people who are afraid of large dogs enjoy the company of your decidedly unintimidating little dog. Shih Tzu are sturdy enough to visit all but very rambunctious kids, and sweet enough to be welcomed by people who are very frail.

If your Shih Tzu is people-oriented and well socialized, he could make a great therapy dog.

Many Shih Tzu are truly gifted at this volunteer work. They seem to sense who needs a gentle snuggle and who wants to be entertained by the breed's famous clownishness. It's an honor to volunteer side-by-side with one of these gifted dogs.

Of course, therapy work isn't for every dog. Just as every person isn't cut out to be a social worker, every dog isn't cut out to be a therapy dog. People who evaluate therapy dogs estimate that about 25 to 30 percent of trained dogs enjoy this work—although that number is probably significantly higher for Shih Tzu. No one wants to be visited by a dog who doesn't like them, so if your dog is grouchy with strangers, he may need more training. If he's got health problems that make touch uncomfortable for him, or if he's shy, this probably isn't the activity for him.

Why Be Certified?

You have a great little dog—but it does cost some money and time to be evaluated and certified by one of the therapy organizations. Thinking of skipping the test? Don't. Most hospitals, nursing homes, and schools require you to be certified.

Plus, the certifying organizations give their therapy dog teams liability insurance as part of your membership. You must have liability coverage if you do this kind of work.

It's also important to find the right niche for each dog. Some Shih Tzu love kids but find older adults boring. Others clearly love to snuggle with older folks but find the less predictable antics of children intimidating. If you work through an animal-assisted therapy group, you and your dog will find a niche you can both enjoy.

Getting Certified as a Therapy Dog

Certification for all therapy dogs starts out with a Canine Good Citizen Test. This test checks for a mastery of basic commands, as well as the dog's ability to work calmly and quietly around people and other animals. The certifying therapy dog organization may modify the test somewhat. For example, all organizations use wheelchairs and walkers during the "walking through a crowd" section of the test, to be sure prospective therapy dogs are comfortable around medical equipment. But some organizations don't require the supervised separation segment of the test, because therapy dogs should always stay on leash with their human partners during therapy visits.

Some organizations also add extensive temperament testing to their requirements. These tests are designed to make sure your prospective therapy dog not only accepts the kinds of challenges he's likely to face in a therapy visit, but will also actually enjoy them. The requirements of the Delta Society test are good ones to practice, no matter which organization certifies you. If you spend much time in any facility, this test evaluates your dog for his response to the following situations:

1 Overall exam (accepting handling)
2 Exuberant and clumsy petting
3 Restraining hug
4 Staggering, gesturing individual
5 Angry yelling
6 Bumped from behind
7 Crowded and petted by several people
8 Leave it (ignore a toy on the floor)
9 Offered a treat (to take gently)

CONFORMATION: THE GLAMOUR EVENT

If you watch dog shows on television, you know that Shih Tzu are always competitive. With their flowing coats, expressive faces, and charming personalities, they are always crowd favorites. The breed certainly earns its fair share of Toy Group wins and even Best-in-Show awards.

The most famous Shih Tzu in the show ring was Ch. Charing Cross Ragtime Cowboy, known to his many fans as "Joey." He holds the record as the top-winning toy dog of all time. Not only did this great dog win 52 Best-in-Show wins in just one year (in 2000), he also won first place in the Toy Group at the Westminster Kennel Club dog show twice (2000 and 2001).

About Conformation

Shih Tzu are judged by how closely they match the breed standard—the blueprint that describes how Shih Tzu look and act. (Dog show competitions are called conformation events because the dog is judge by how closely he *conforms* to the breed standard.)

The dog show world is competitive, but those who do it love it.

Knowing the intricacies of grooming for the show ring is critical if you want to compete in it.

Judges look for:

Breed Type

Shih Tzu have defining characteristics, such as their flowing coats and expressive faces. These defining characteristics are important in keeping Shih Tzu distinct from other breeds. In the Shih Tzu ring, these characteristics include details such as the dog's height, proportions, coat texture, tail set, and eyes.

Structure

Winning Shih Tzu are physically sound and have a level topline, a strong and straight gait, and general heartiness.

Temperament

The Shih Tzu standard includes a more detailed description of the breed's personality than perhaps any other dog breed standard. It says, "As the sole purpose of the Shih Tzu is that of a companion and house pet, it is essential that its temperament be outgoing, happy, affectionate, friendly, and trusting towards all." A great show dog will exude that wonderful Shih Tzu personality.

Ideally, a show dog has the whole package—breed type, great structure, and the wonderful Shih Tzu temperament.

Showing a Shih Tzu

The grooming requirements for a show Shih Tzu are somewhat mind-numbing. Even though the dogs are primped and preened at the show, the commitment to keeping that glorious show coat is a 365-day-a-year job.

The skill of the handler makes a difference in the ring, too. Show dogs are gaited at the pace that shows off their movement to its best advantage. They're taught to stand still in a perfect show pose (called *stacking*) on both a table, where they're examined by the judge, and on the floor.

The star of the dog show is the dog—not the handler. Still, it's important for handlers to look professional, so exhibitors usually wear business attire (even when the show is being held at a country fair ground or outside in a field). People usually pick a color that will complement the looks of the dog when he's on the table being examined by the judge.

If you're interested in showing your own dog, ask your local kennel club about conformation classes. In class, you'll learn about gaiting and stacking your dog, as well as etiquette in the show ring.

Many Shih Tzu fanciers hire professional handlers to show their dogs.

Showing in the United States

Dog shows are an elimination tournament with one ultimate winner—the Best-in-Show dog.

In each breed, males (called *dogs* in competition parlance) who aren't yet champions compete against each other in several classes. The winner of each class competes against the other winners for the honor of Winners Dog.

The females (*bitches* in dog show lingo) also compete in their own classes, and the winners of those classes compete against each other for Winners Bitch.

The Winners Dog and the Winners Bitch earn points toward their championships. Points are awarded based on how many

Show dogs often live a life on the road, traveling to shows to earn points toward a championship.

Show Dogs Come From Show Dog Stock

Show dogs are bred for generations to conform to the breed standard. Don't expect to buy a puppy with championship potential from someone who doesn't show her dogs.

other dogs the winner has beaten that day. They can earn 1 to 5 points. To become a champion, a dog must earn a total of 15 points, and some of those points must be gained from at least two *major* wins (shows with enough competition to award at least 3 points for a win).

The final class in the breed is the Specials class, in which the dogs who are already champions, as well as the Winners Dog and Winners Bitch, compete with each other for Best of Breed.

In the United States, Shih Tzu are in the Toy Group. The Best-of-Breed Shih Tzu eventually competes with other members of the Toy Group by coming up against the Best-of-Breed Yorkshire Terrier, Pug, Pekingese, Pomeranian, and other toy dogs. How does the judge compare a Shih Tzu with a Chihuahua or a Maltese? At the group level, the dogs aren't directly compared with each other; they are compared with how well they match their own breed standards. So, if the Shih Tzu comes closer to the Shih Tzu standard than the Maltese comes to the Maltese standard, the Shih Tzu wins.

The winner of the Toy Group competes against the winners from the other groups (Sporting, Hound, Terrier, Working, Non-Sporting, and Herding) for Best in Show.

Showing in England

Shows in Britain are very similar to dog shows in the United States, but they also have some important differences.

There's one very major difference for Shih Tzu fanciers: In the United Kingdom, Shih Tzu are shown in the Utility Group (equivalent to the Non-Sporting Group in America), where Bulldogs, Dalmatians, Lhasa Apsos, and other dogs who don't neatly fit into other categories are shown. In the United States, Shih Tzu are shown in the Toy Group.

The biggest general difference between American dog shows and English shows is the difficulty of gaining a championship title. It's a much more difficult task in England. In English championship shows, the top male (dog) and top female (bitch) are awarded challenge certificates (CC). It takes three CCs to become a champion. Unlike in America, the English shows don't have separate competition for dogs who aren't yet champions, so a Shih Tzu has to beat dogs who are already champions to earn a CC. This is a very difficult task, because English shows

You may not think of your Shih Tzu as a "performer," but like a lot of dogs, he may blossom with the training and fun that's to be had participating in certain events.

are very large and extremely competitive.

A Shih Tzu has to beat the very best other Shih Tzu to earn a championship in England, which makes the title all the more respected.

DOG SPORTS AND THE ADVENTUROUS SHIH TZU

Okay, the average Shih Tzu is built for comfort, not so much for speed. Still, your little dog is one of the finest companion dogs on the face of the planet, and with today's modern, positive training methods, he can do well—and even excel—at some dog sports.

It's also important to remember that, although many Shih Tzu are couch potatoes, others have a lot more energy than you might expect. These busier little guys need a hobby to keep them focused. The answer for those dogs is one of the dog sports.

Adventurous Shih Tzu have hit the top ranks in three major dog spots: rally obedience, competitive obedience, and agility. Also, some less well-known sports can be a lot of fun, including flyball, freestyle (dancing with dogs), and even tracking.

Here's a taste of the dog sports that your little guy would love to try:

If you start working with your dog when he's a pup, he will easily learn simple things like retrieving that can be useful later on in competitive obedience.

Rally Obedience

In 2005, the AKC approved a new dog sport: rally obedience. If you're dreaming of competing in agility or obedience, or just want to have a lot of fun with your little dog, rally obedience is a great place to start.

The judge lays out a course with signs that tell the dog and handler what to do. The judge may use 40 different signs. The commands are fun, such as heeling backwards for three steps, weaving through cones with your dog, and turning in circles.

It's a sport of fun teamwork—you're encouraged to talk with your dog when you're on the course. Rally is spontaneous, because you never know what the course will be from one competition to the next. It also reinforces your dog's obedience skills, such as heeling, sitting, and lying down.

The dogs are judged on how well they complete the course, and ties are broken by the dogs who complete the course in the fastest time. So, dogs and owners go through the course as fast as they can, which makes a dog's tail wag with excitement.

It can take years of training for a dog to be ready to compete in agility or traditional obedience. Rally, on the other hand, relies on the combination of a few basic commands that most people learn in dog-training classes. Once you learn what the signs mean, even young dogs and inexperienced handlers can enjoy the sport.

Rally also teaches skills, such as precise heeling, that will be useful if you decide to continue training in competitive obedience. It also gets the dogs used to weaving and circling, which are skills your dog can use in agility. Try it—you and your Shih Tzu will have a lot of fun.

Rally Novice, the first level of rally competition, is always done on-leash, and the course includes 10 to 15 stations. After passing the Rally Novice Class at three shows, your dog earns his Rally Novice (RN) title.

The Rally Advanced class is more challenging, because dogs are off-leash and have 12 to 17 stations. Dogs earn the title of RA (Rally Advanced).

The most challenging level is the Rally Excellent class. The course has 15 to 20 stations, and dogs earn the title of RE (Rally Excellent).

Once your dog has his RE title, he can try for the title of Rally Advanced Excellent (RAE). To earn this title, your dog must pass both the advanced course and the excellent course at 10 different trials.

The Agility Preferred Class

The AKC now gives titles in the "preferred class," which has lower jump heights and more generous course times. This is a good option for older dogs, because it allows them to still compete and earn titles.

Agility

Does your active little Shih Tzu love to run, jump, and romp? Then maybe agility is the sport for you.

In this fast-paced competition, dogs run through an obstacle course, leaping over hurdles (set as low as 8 inches [20.3 cm] for small dogs), climbing up A-frames, slaloming through weave poles, and zooming through aboveground tunnels.

Agility Competition

The dogs go through a course that is either a *standard course*, which has a number of contact obstacles (such as A-frames, seesaws, or dog walks), plus items such as weave poles, a pause table (where dogs have to Stay to show control), tire jumps, and tunnels. The *Jumpers with Weaves* class doesn't have contact obstacles or a pause table, which slow the dog down. This is a very fast course.

Dogs progress from novice level, to open, to excellent level competition. At each level, the courses are tougher, with more obstacles to navigate and more complicated courses to run.

In AKC competitions, dogs earn the titles NA and NAJ

A Shih Tzu Who Moves at the Speed of Sound

In February of 1999, the AKC added the title of Master Agility Champion (MACH). Most of the dogs who have earned this title have been speedy breeds, such as Border Collies, Shelties, or Papillons.

One Shih Tzu decided to beat the odds.

In 2003, Harper's Naughty Niki was the first Shih Tzu to achieve this difficult, demanding, and prestigious title. Other dogs are following in this dog's jet stream. One could be yours. The dog's official title as of November 2005: MACH 4 Harper's Naughty Niki CD RN. What do those initials mean? It means this amazing dog has met the tough qualifications for a MACH title four times over. That's a huge achievement even at the very top levels of the sport. The CD is an obedience title and RN is a rally obedience title. This is one accomplished little dog!

(Novice Agility and Novice Jumpers with Weaves), OA and OAJ (Open Agility and Open Jumpers with Weaves), AX and AXJ (Excellent Agility and Excellent Jumpers with Weaves), and MX and MXJ (Master Agility and Master Jumpers with Weaves).

The most elite dogs earn the highly respected title of MACH—Master Agility Champion. The dogs at this level complete courses flawlessly at top speed. It's no wonder that MACH reminds us of top-gun jet pilots who go faster than the speed of sound! Dogs who master this level multiple times are called MACH 1, MACH 2, MACH 3, and so on.

Finding an Agility Class

Even if you never consider competing, you and your dog should consider taking an agility class. It's a great opportunity for you and your Shih Tzu to go out and have a terrific time together.

The number one consideration in an agility class is safety. This is one of the few sports that can result in serious injuries. Falling off an A-frame or dog walk can break bones. Neglecting to warm up before jumping can cause serious muscle injuries.

Out-of-control dogs who are off-leash can also hurt other dogs.

Before you sign up for a class, visit a class in action. Does the trainer emphasize safety? Are the larger dogs under control? If the answers are "yes," sign up! You and your Shih Tzu will have a great time together.

Competitive Obedience

Shih Tzu are one of the world's best companion dogs. Using today's modern training methods, you and your little buddy can excel at the sport of obedience.

Obedience competition starts out with the basic commands of Heel, Stay, Come, Sit, and Down. As the levels of competition increase, additional skills are required—retrieving, jumping, hand signals, and even finding objects only by scent. Shih Tzu have mastered all these skills—yours might be able to, too!

Additional Titles

But wait! There's more. The very best dogs can keep competing for more titles.

Utility dogs who go on competing and pass *both* Open and Utility at 10 shows after they earn their UD titles will earn the Utility Dog Excellent (UDX) title.

In these classes, which are limited to dogs with advanced titles, dogs earn points by defeating other dogs, on a designated scale. After a dog earns 100 points, he earns the highest title in obedience—Obedience Trial Champion (OTCH).

Competitive Obedience Exercises

To earn an obedience title, the dog must pass every exercise at three different dog shows. At the Novice level, dogs earn a Companion Dog (CD) title. Open dogs earn a Companion Dog Excellent (CDX). Utility dogs earn a Utility Dog (UD) title. Check out the AKC website (www.akc.org) for information on rules and requirements. The United Kennel Club (UKC) also holds obedience trials around the country, with rules similar to those of the AKC's. To learn more about UKC competitions, go to their website at www.ukcdogs.com.

Tracking

The AKC holds tracking events that any purebred can enter. If you and your Shih Tzu enjoy spending time outdoors, you might just find this is a good event to try. Although Shih Tzu are at a bit of a disadvantage with their short noses (it's easier to follow a scent if you've got a big nose like a Bloodhound or Basset), there are certainly Shih Tzu who would love to learn the sport.

If your Shih Tzu enjoys the outdoors, you may want to give tracking a try.

The Cookie Monster

A Shih Tzu with a name like Itsy Bitsy Cookie Monster doesn't sound like a dog who could outsmart Border Collies. But that's just what Bitsy did.

Bitsy is the first Obedience Trial Champion Shih Tzu. She earned the last points to gain this coveted title when she beat a Border Collie in a run-off. (When two dogs earn an identical score in an obedience competition, they go in the ring for a run-off. The judge gives the dog and handler a heeling pattern, and the team that does the work most precisely wins. It's heart-racing to watch the perfect footwork of the dogs and handlers as two top competitors perform.)

Her official name: OTCH Itsy Bitsy Cookie Monster UDX 3. The OTCH stands for "Obedience Trial Champion," and the UDX 3 means that she's qualified for the highly respected and difficult-to-achieve UDX title three times over!

Oh, and if you think it's too late to train your dog, you can get even more inspiration from Itsy. She was a rescue dog, and her owner, Mary Baker, didn't adopt Bitsy until the dog was about 4 or 5 years old. It turns out you *can* teach an older dog new tricks. And clever Bitsy proved that a little dog who was once just another face in a rescue could be a true star.

Tracking requires a dog to follow a scent trail left by a human. The sport is usually taught in a way that would appeal to any Shih Tzu—laying a little trail of treats for the dog to follow. In this sport, the dog does the leading, and the human does the following. In fact, the mantra of tracking is: Trust Your Dog. Even if you don't get far in the sport, it's fun to take your dog outside and explore the world of scent together.

Tracking tests are all pass-or-fail, noncompetitive events that celebrate the instinct of your dog and the bond of trust between the human and the dog. Dogs earn the titles of Tracking Dog and Tracking Dog Excellent, with courses that are between 440 and 1,000 yards long. The dogs follow a weaving scent trail laid down by one person. Advanced-work classes add obstacles to cross and confusing scent trails, laid down by people who cross the path of the person the dog is tracking. The Variable Surface Tracking test involves tracking in urban areas. Dogs who earn all these titles are crowned Champion Tracker. Only a handful of dogs of any breed (and no Shih Tzu) have earned the title of Champion Tracker.

For more information on tracking, go to the AKC website at www.akc.org.

Flyball

Flyball is something of "extreme sport" for dogs. It's a relay race where dogs fly over a series of four hurdles. They hit a box that tosses a ball to them, and then they race back over the hurdles with the ball. All this is done at warp speed.

Every flyball team wants one short dog on the team, because the whole team gets to jump shorter hurdles if they have a small member. There may be a team looking for your speedy Shih Tzu.

Check out this incredibly fast-paced sport at the North

American Flyball website at www.flyball.org.

Dancing With Dogs

Do you like music? Imagine a sport in which you move in time to your favorite music while your dog does tricks with you. That's the new sport of Canine Freestyle—dancing with dogs. You pick the music and the costumes that suit you and your Shih Tzu. While many dog sports require speed and athleticism from dogs (and even their humans), freestyle allows you to build a routine that suits the natural pace of your team. It's a wonderful sport for a dog with a more deliberate pace, and it is suited to older dogs as well as younger ones.

For more information, go to the World Canine Freestyle Organization's website at www.worldcaninefreestyle.org.

The Indefinite Listing Privilege

If you have a purebred Shih Tzu who isn't registered, you can still enter every AKC event except for conformation.

Go to the AKC website at www.akc.org and check out the requirements for an Indefinite Listing Privilege (ILP). You fill out some forms and send them in, and you and your dog will have a chance to compete.

TRICKS AND GAMES

Because Shih Tzu are so good at sitting on laps and looking adorable, it's easy to forget to challenge their clever brains. Your little Shih Tzu loves you and wants more than anything else to spend time interacting with you. Your dog needs activities that will keep his mind alert and strengthen the already strong bond you have together. Give him the chance by teaching him tricks and playing games.

Here are a few ideas to get you started:

Tricks

Shih Tzu have an innate sense of humor that makes them perfect dogs for performing tricks. Select tricks that use your dog's natural talents and give him big rewards when he does them. He'll love showing off to your family and friends.

The Shih Tzu's intelligence and sense of humor make him an excellent candidate for some easy trick training.

Sad Dog!

No sight on earth is sadder than a sad look on a Shih Tzu's face. This trick uses the "awwwww" factor of that adorable expression.

When you think of Lassie looking sad, what does he do? He lies down

Trick Safety

Be careful what you ask your dog to do. Dogs will seldom injure themselves when they play, but many dogs will do whatever you ask—even if it hurts. Dogs under one year of age should never be required to jump on command. Any command that requires physical strain should first include a warm-up of running or playing to make sure your pooch doesn't pull a muscle or otherwise injure himself. Remember: No trick is as important as your dog's comfort and safety!

on the floor and looks up with those soulful eyes. Your Shih Tzu can put Lassie to shame on this trick!

First, your dog needs to learn a reliable Down command from the last chapter. Then, hold a cookie on the floor—when your greedy little dog puts his head down to get the treat, say "Sad dog" in a quiet, slow voice that stretches out the syllables. If you keep your voice low and slow, he's likely to keep his head down. If you make your voice happy and high, he's likely to look up. Keep giving him treats as long as he keeps his head down.

If your dog doesn't understand what you're asking for, place him on a chair (life is easier with little dogs!) and put the treat below the edge of the chair. Position him so that his chin rests on the edge of the chair when he's reaching down for the treat.

Walk Like a Man

With his adorable little round face, your dog already looks like a more dignified version of a human. How about teaching him the trick of Walk Like a Man?

While your dog is standing, hold a treat up a few inches (cm) above your dog's nose. When he reaches up to get the treat, give it to him and tell him he's a brilliant boy!

Once he stands well on his feet, hold the treat in front of him, and teach him to walk a step.

Do be careful. This trick requires the dog to develop muscles he doesn't normally use. Do just a step or two at first, and then gradually work your way up to several steps. This is *not* an appropriate trick for Shih Tzu with back or joint problems.

Still, it's a fun trick for most Shih Tzu, who really do look like little bears or humans when they "walk."

Wave, Shake, and Gimme Five

It's easy and fun to teach your Shih Tzu to wave, shake, and "gimme five." All three tricks are based on the same motion.

It's a great trick for all dogs—especially therapy dogs. Your little therapy dog can break the ice with clients by waving to them, or he can wave "goodbye" as he leaves a hospital room.

- **Wave.** Let your Shih Tzu see you put a treat in your hand, then wrap the treat in your fist. Hold your fist near your dog's paws. Soon, your dog will start pawing at your fist,

Routine grooming can be a training opportunity.

demanding the treat. This is a time to reward his pushy behavior!

As soon as he scratches at your hand, say "Good wave!" and give him the treat. Soon, you can put your fist near him, say "Wave!" and he'll paw at you. Now he's figured out the basics!

The next step is to tell him to "Sit," and hold your fist just a bit out of reach. He'll have to reach out with his paw. He's waving!

Over time, hold your hand farther and farther away. You can also gradually change the fist into a waving hand.

- **Gimme Five.** Teach your dog to give you a high five after he's learned to wave. When he waves, put your palm on his pads and say "Gimme five!"

  Your dog will be a hip dude in a matter of minutes, since this is really just waving with a twist.
- **Shake**. Okay, "high five" may be a little too California surf-style for some dogs. If your little dog is more the corporate executive type, teach Shake.

  When your dog is very sure of himself on the wave, reach

Entertain your Shih Tzu with a game like hide-and-seek.

out and gently take his paw and say "Good shake." Give him a big treat right away, so that he thinks shaking is fun.

Games in the House

Games are interactive fun for both of you—and for other members of the family.

Try these, and then think up some of your own!

Find Dad!

Well, find Dad, or Mom, Aunt Sue, or your son or daughter—anyone your dog sees regularly. Start by sitting down with two people—let's call them Joe and Jane. Jane says, "Find Joe!" and Joe shows the dog he has a treat. When the dog comes to eat the treat, tell him he's wonderful! Then, Jane holds a treat, and Joe says, "Find Jane!" The clever Shih Tzu merrily goes to her—and gets a treat. Gradually, Joe and Jane get farther apart from each other until they are eventually around the corner from each other.

Soon, one of them can go into another room, and they can send the dog to find each other. They can even send messages to each other via the dog!

Where's Waldo?

Teach your dog the names of his toys. This works especially well for the Shih Tzu who loves to collect and sit on his little group of favorite toys. Throw the red ball and say "Get the ball." If he likes playing with his toys, he'll happily go to his ball.

Later, throw the stuffed mouse and say "Get mousie!" Always use the names of his toys when you give them to him. Most—but not all—dogs learn the names of their favorite toys.

You can amuse each other endlessly! Tell your dog to "Get his mousie" and then play together. Or tell him to get his ball and then play with him. Tell him to get his panda toy or his froggy toy. It goes on and on.

Clean the House!

Who says Shih Tzu aren't working dogs? Yours can help clean the house!

If your dog likes to play fetching games, and if you've taught him *Drop It* (from Chapter 6), you have a perfect helper. Ask him to pick up a toy, and then clap your hands and have him follow you to a basket or toy storage bin. Then tell him "Drop it" and give him lots of praise and treats when he drops the toy in the basket. Once he understands the game, you can show him socks you want him to pick up. He'll be better than a housekeeper. Well, at least cuter than one!

Your Shih Tzu will learn new skills throughout his lifetime, just as humans do. He'll have a happier, more interesting life if you continue to give him new challenges. Whether it's serious competition or just games around the house, continuing to stimulate your dog with learning new things will be good for both of you. You'll end up with a lifetime bond and a lifetime of memories.

Chapter 8

HEALTH of Your Shih Tzu

Don't let this chapter panic you. Shih Tzu, like most small dogs, often live very long lives. Their average life span is 10 to 14 years, but many far outlive that range.

The best way you can help ensure that your very special little dog will enjoy many years with you is to be aware of his health. This includes providing the best preventive care, as well as understanding the health issues that affect Shih Tzu. An informed owner almost always translates into a healthy pup.

This chapter helps give you the tools to help your wonderful little buddy live a long, healthy, vibrant life.

FINDING A VETERINARIAN

Veterinarians are an extraordinary group of professionals. It can be just as hard to get into veterinary school as it is to get into medical school—and a veterinarian's reward is lower pay and patients who just might bite if they aren't happy.

As in other medical professions, some veterinarians are more skilled than are others. Still, the biggest difference between one veterinarian and another is style. Let's face it—you want a veterinarian who treats your little dog as a family member, not as "just a dog." You want someone who will take the time to talk with you and explain what issues your Shih Tzu is facing and what options are available.

The most skilled veterinarian on the planet won't do your Shih Tzu much good if she doesn't communicate well. Look for a veterinarian who has a personal style that makes you feel welcome and makes you feel a part of the support team for your dog.

Get a Referral

If your breeder lives in your community, and you respect her, ask which veterinarian she uses for her Shih Tzu. Also, people who work in dog professions often know local veterinarians well. If you already have a groomer or a trainer you respect but are still looking for a great veterinarian, ask these professionals who they recommend.

Good Veterinarians Are Communicators

Communication is the most important skill for a veterinarian. If your veterinarian isn't a good communicator in an office visit, just think how difficult communication will be during the course of a long illness or in a medical emergency.

If your friends love their dogs just as much as you love yours, they may also have searched for a great veterinarian. Ask them who they go to.

Go for a Visit

Selecting a veterinarian is just as intensely personal as choosing a doctor. The ideal veterinarian for your friend's Great Dane might not be as well suited to your Shih Tzu. We all have different reactions to different personalities—the veterinarian your neighbor thinks is efficient can strike you as cold or curt. The only way you can decide if a veterinarian is right for you is to make an appointment and pay a visit. Veterinarians welcome this effort—it shows how much you care about your dog—and the staff should be proud to show off their facilities. Here's what to look for:

- **Cleanliness**. From front office to back rooms, the entire facility should be gleaming with cleanliness.
- **Love of animals.** People who work there should love animals. Expect to see them talking gently to their four-legged patients and touching them soothingly.
- **Answers your questions.** The veterinarian and her staff should be glad to answer your questions.
- **Experience with small dogs.** A veterinarian who has many other Shih Tzu and other small dogs in the practice will have an extra empathy for your concerns. (Bonus points if the veterinarian owns a small-size dog.) Subtle and not-so-subtle differences come into play between caring for a 10-pound (4.5-kg) dog and a 100-pound dog (45.4-kg) (or a 1,000-pound [453.6-kg] horse).
- **Convenient hours.** Arrangements for after-hour or weekend emergency needs should be convenient for you. In small towns, local veterinarians may take turns being on-call during off-hours. Larger cities are likely to have emergency veterinary clinics staffed by specialists. Find out what provisions your veterinarian recommends if your dog needs help when the clinic is closed for the night.
- **Modern anesthetics.** The veterinarian should always use one of the modern gas anesthetics. Shih Tzu, like other small dogs and flat-faced breeds, can be sensitive to anesthesia. Modern gas anesthetics, such as isoflurane, are

much safer than the old-fashioned intravenous anesthetics. Be sure that your veterinarian always uses one of the new products.

- **Modern surgical equipment.** The veterinarian should use the latest equipment to monitor patients during surgery. Dogs are put under general anesthesia much more often than people are. Your Shih Tzu is likely to experience anesthesia several times in his life—when he's altered, for annual teeth cleaning, and sometimes for X-rays. Your veterinarian should have equipment, much like a surgeon has, to continuously monitor your Shih Tzu's heart functions and other vital functions.
- **Certified vet technicians.** The best veterinarians use certified veterinary technicians to assist in surgery, do dental cleanings, and administer anesthesia. Certified vet techs take a rigorous 2- or 4-year college program that is equivalent to a nursing degree. They then have to pass a tough test to earn their certifications. These are respected professionals in any veterinary team. Don't settle for a veterinary practice that doesn't hire the best staff.
- **AAHA certification.** Veterinary practices can voluntarily ask the American Animal Hospital Association (AAHA) to send in trained consultants who determine if the clinic meets their standards. Although many excellent veterinary hospitals don't participate in the certification program, it is one indication of a commitment to quality care for your Shih Tzu.
- **Sufficient appointment time.** The clinic allows plenty of time for your appointment. If you want to learn about your dog's health and use your veterinarian's expertise, you need enough time in the office to discuss your pet. Practices vary: Some schedule routine appointments for as little as every 10 minutes, while others allow as much as a half hour.

Take the time and trouble to find a veterinarian who you trust to take your dog's health as seriously as you do.

Your veterinarian will want to examine your puppy thoroughly to look and feel for anything suspicious.

- **Referrals to specialty clinics.** The best veterinarians don't hesitate to refer animals to specialty clinics. One of the big stories in veterinary medicine in the last decade has been the growth of veterinary specialists, such as cardiologists, internal medicine specialists, ophthalmologists, cancer specialists, orthopedic surgeons, and neurologists. The best general-practice veterinarians, like the best general-practice human doctors, quickly refer their patients to a specialist when specialized knowledge or equipment might improve an animal's quality of care.

YOUR SHIH TZU'S FIRST VET VISIT

Your Shih Tzu should have his first veterinary visit within 48 hours of his arrival home. It's important to be sure that he's arrived healthy and well and, if he hasn't, to find out what you must do.

Your veterinarian will take a thorough look from nose to tail—and everything in between. She will listen to your dog's heart and lungs, palpate his tummy, and look for abnormalities in his eyes. She will inspect teeth and gums and look for swelling in your dog's glands. You'll probably be asked to bring a stool sample so that your veterinarian can check for worms. She may do a blood test, especially if your dog looks unwell or if you have adopted a rescue dog.

Making Veterinary Visits Pleasant

Believe it or not, your Shih Tzu can learn to love his trips to the veterinarian's office. It just takes a positive attitude from you, some preparation, and some treats.

Occasionally, stop by your veterinarian's office for fun. Yes—for fun. Bring your Shih Tzu in to the waiting area and give him some treats. Ask the office staff to give him some cookies, too. Then go home. If your Shih Tzu has fun most of the time when he goes to the vet and only sometimes gets poked and prodded, he'll decide he likes this place.

When you bring your dog in for exams, bring his favorite cookies with you. Make every visit, even serious ones, a little bit of a party. Think how much more you'd like going to your doctor if you got a tasty dessert every time you went!

One reason that veterinary visits are traumatic to a dog is because he is poked and prodded in ways that never happen anywhere else. Help your dog by acclimating him to being routinely touched all over. You can practice looking inside your dog's mouth and checking his teeth. Say "Lips," and then touch his lips and give him a treat. When this becomes routine for him, pull up his lips and say "Teeth." When he gets to the veterinarian's office, he won't be worried and intimidated when his mouth and teeth are inspected.

A stethoscope is a scary contraption to a dog. Get your Shih Tzu ready for his exams by regularly touching him at home with a variety of objects, including plastic bags, spoons, and crinkled aluminum foil. When he gets to the vet's office, a cold metal and plastic stethoscope won't seem odd to him.

Evaluating Your Veterinarian

Your initial well-pet exam is a good time to think about whether the veterinarian you've chosen is the right vet for you and your dog. Is the veterinarian gentle with your small dog? Does she communicate well with you? Did you leave feeling good about the experience?

VACCINES: PROTECTING YOUR SHIH TZU AGAINST DISEASE

Your Shih Tzu puppy will be vaccinated against diseases that used to kill thousands of dogs a year. Canine distemper used to rage through kennels, shelters, and neighborhoods. Parvo killed almost every dog who contracted it. With today's medical miracles, if you purchase a puppy from a responsible breeder, and then correctly vaccinate your dog, you will never have to worry about these diseases.

Even something as seemingly simple as vaccination against disease is a balancing act. Some vaccines are more effective than

Vaccinations are necessary to protect the long-term health of your Shih Tzu. Discuss a vaccine protocol with your veterinarian that suits your individual dog.

others in preventing disease, and some vaccines have more side effects than others. There is a great deal of controversy about how often—if ever—dogs need to get booster shots for their vaccines.

Discuss your dog's vaccinations with your veterinarian. Every dog is unique. Different parts of the country and different lifestyles also matter. If you travel with your dog, for example, he may be exposed to diseases that he might not come in contact with at home.

Here are the latest recommendations for vaccinating your Shih Tzu, but keep in mind that your veterinarian may suggest slightly different protocols for your individual dog.

The Core Vaccines

Every puppy should have vaccinations for rabies, parvovirus, distemper, and adenovirus-2 (which also protects against canine infectious hepatitis). These diseases are still widespread, they can be deadly if the animal comes down with the illness, and the vaccines have very low likelihood of side effects.

Puppies get their first shots when they're about 6 to 8 weeks old. Until then, they receive immunity from disease through their mother's milk. After your puppy is weaned, vaccinations give your dog his own immunity. Puppy vaccines are given in a series between the ages of about 6 weeks and 4 months. Dogs receive booster shots 1 year later.

Optional Vaccines

Your veterinarian might also recommend vaccines against other diseases, depending on where you live and your lifestyle. For example, Lyme disease is common in some areas of the country and not in others. Leptospirosis is a concern in some areas, but the disease hasn't been reported for decades in other parts of the country. Bordetella (kennel cough) is a flu-like illness your dog may be exposed to if you board him or take him to dog shows, but it may not be a concern if you don't take him to places where large numbers of other dogs are present.

If your veterinarian recommends these vaccines, be sure to discuss the reasons why your Shih Tzu should—or shouldn't—have them.

Puppies and Veterinary Offices

Remember that veterinary offices are places where people bring their sick animals. Although veterinarians clean and disinfect their offices scrupulously, it's always a good idea to hold your dog on your lap in the waiting area, especially if you have a puppy who hasn't completed his vaccinations yet.

Special Vaccination Concerns for Small-Breed Dogs

One vaccine that is of special concern to people with small dogs is the leptospirosis vaccine. Leptospirosis is a serious disease that can be a real danger to dogs in certain parts of the country. However, the leptospirosis vaccine has a high rate of reported severe anaphylactic shock—an allergic reaction in which your dog could stop breathing and even die. If your veterinarian recommends this vaccine, carefully discuss the pros and cons before making a decision.

The Booster Controversy

For decades, dogs were given their puppy vaccines, and then given booster shots against all the major diseases every year. The best owners gave their dogs the most shots!

But then problems began to arise that have been attributed to vaccines and overvaccinating. Giving too many vaccinations may actually overstress an animal's immune system, rather than strengthen it. Health issues, from seizures to a variety of autoimmune disorders, may be linked to giving too many vaccines over the course of a dog's lifetime.

A major change in vaccine recommendations came about when veterinarians started noticing some problems in cats. In 1998, concerns about increased rates of a certain kind of cancer

A dog's lifestyle can influence which shots he receives and how often. Show dogs have unique stressors, as do dogs who frequent the outdoors.

in cats at vaccine-injection sites were reported in the *Journal of the American Veterinary Medical Association.* Later studies showed that between 1 in 1,000 and 1 in 10,000 cats develop cancer at their vaccination sites. Current research is trying to determine exactly which vaccines are most likely to cause this reaction and if the problem is caused by the vaccine itself or the ingredients that are mixed with the vaccine.

Changing Vaccination Protocols

Veterinarians are still trying to decide where to draw the line on the number and frequency of vaccines to make sure dogs and cats are well protected from serious diseases without overvaccinating. Part of the problem is that no one knows for sure how long a vaccine's immunity lasts. One year? Three years? Ten years? Forever?

Scientists at veterinary schools around the country are conducting long-range studies to determine how long a vaccination will protect your dog against disease, so in the future, recommended vaccine protocols may change.

Vaccinations: Leave Them to the Professionals

It's tempting to think about saving some money by giving your Shih Tzu vaccinations at home. After all, countless vaccine products are available from pet supply catalogs and Internet sites. This can be a serious mistake.

Vaccines aren't "one size fits all" medications. Do you choose a multi-virus vaccine, or vaccinate against one disease at a time? Do you know whether your Shih Tzu would be better off with a modified live vaccine or a killed version? The answers can vary, depending on the age, size, and general health of your dog.

Many veterinarians believe that not all vaccine brands are the same quality. Bulk vaccines are cheaper, but most veterinarians agree that single-shot packages provide better quality control and have less chance of adverse side effects.

These kinds of decisions are best made by a knowledgeable, caring, helpful professional who knows the needs of your dog. Vaccinations at a veterinarian's office are worth every penny they cost.

Keep Abreast of the Latest Vaccine Protocols

With recommendations about vaccines being in a state of flux, it's more important than ever to keep a close relationship with your veterinarian. She will be abreast of the latest research on the subject and can help you make the right decisions for your dog.

Current Recommendations for Vaccine Frequency

Currently, most veterinary schools in the United States recommend that all puppies receive a series of core vaccines between the ages of 6 weeks and 4 months of age, with boosters a year later. Boosters should be given every 1 to 3 years after the initial booster. Boosters of any kind are still controversial and, after more studies are complete, it's possible there will be recommendations for fewer boosters—and maybe none.

Don't forget your annual veterinary visit, even if your dog doesn't need a booster shot. Remember, a year in the life of a dog is roughly equivalent to 7 human years. Your dog's annual exam is the chance to head off a disease before it becomes serious. Your veterinarian should listen to your dog's heart and lungs, examine his eyes, check for patellar luxation, feel his skin for lumps and bumps, compare his weight to what it was a year before, and make sure you're on the right track. Don't lose the opportunity to have this care for your dog, no matter what you decide about booster shots.

ALTERING YOUR SHIH TZU

It can be upsetting to take your sweet little Shih Tzu puppy to the veterinarian to be altered. After all, your little guy is just a kid—and he has to undergo general anesthesia. But you're doing the right thing when you make this decision.

The Benefits of Spaying

No one has pink ribbon campaigns for them, but breast cancer is a leading cause of death in female dogs. The American Kennel Club Canine Health Foundation reports that the incidence of mammary tumors in female dogs is almost three times higher than it is in human women, and most canine mammary tumors are malignant. A female dog who hasn't been spayed by the time she is 2 years old has a 50 times greater risk of mammary tumors than a dog who has been spayed before

Unless a show career is in your Shih Tzu's future, having him or her altered is best for your dog.

she comes into her first heat cycle. Female dogs can develop ovarian cancer, which is prevented by spaying. Unspayed females can also develop pyometra, a painful, dangerous, and sometimes fatal uterine infection.

The Benefits of Neutering

Castrating male dogs prevents testicular cancer. It's especially important to alter males whose testicles haven't descended. A puppy's testicles normally descend from his abdomen into his scrotum. However, it's fairly common for testicles in male toy dogs to fail to descend. Testicles that stay in the abdomen are much more likely to become cancerous. This requires your veterinarian to open up his abdomen, making the surgery more like a spay than a neuter.

For male dogs, the desire to roam is often greatly reduced with altering. In fact, dogs who leave home seeking romance are in very serious danger of being injured or killed by cars. In addition, any Shih Tzu who finds himself a stray in the neighborhood may never be returned to you—someone is likely to "rescue" him and keep him as a pet.

Male urine marking is significantly reduced when dogs are neutered. Shih Tzu can be hard to housetrain, and the last thing you want is a male dog who lifts his leg to mark his territory in your home! Male dogs who are altered as puppies are less likely to mark their territories. Even neutering your dog at a later age can be helpful. One study found that about 25 percent of males dogs stop almost all of their territorial marking after altering, and about 60 percent reduce their marking behavior by more than half. You and your carpets will be glad that your boy is altered!

The Safety of Spay and Neutering Surgery

It's normal to worry when you have your dog altered. After

all, you love your dog. The good news is that spaying and castrating are very safe procedures. Although all surgery has some risk, the odds of a long, healthy life for your Shih Tzu are much better if your pet is altered than if you keep your dog intact. Remember, tens of millions of dogs alive and wagging their tails in the United States today have had totally uneventful spay and castration surgeries. Expect yours to be one of them.

Recovery time after alteration is usually only a couple of days. Most likely, your hardest job as a loving owner will be to keep your playful Shih Tzu quiet and restrained for as long as your veterinarian wants you to!

It's a Myth

People fear that their dogs will get fat and lazy after they've been altered. This is a silly myth. Dogs become overweight because they eat too much and exercise too little, not because they've had surgery. Your little Shih Tzu will be just as sweet, funny, and smart as he was before surgery.

When to Spay or Neuter Your Shih Tzu

The right time for your dog to be altered is a medical decision that you and your veterinarian will make together. Most Shih Tzu are altered when they're about 6 months old.

Rescue groups now routinely alter even tiny puppies at very young ages, and it's been found to be just as safe as waiting until later for surgery. If a puppy weighs at least 2 pounds (0.9 kg) and is healthy, veterinarians familiar with early alteration procedures may perform the operation on dogs as young as 6 weeks old.

For the health of your female dog, it is advisable that she be spayed before she comes into her first heat cycle. Going through heat cycles increases her chance of getting dangerous mammary tumors.

Good Reasons Not to Breed

Of course you love your Shih Tzu. After all, you have the most wonderful dog in the world. Even though your dog is practically perfect, it's not a good idea to breed your pet. Here are some things to keep in mind:

Financial Costs

Forget making money on a litter—you'll be lucky to break even. Shih Tzu are one of the most popular breeds in the world, and there's a lot of demand for Shih Tzu puppies. It's easy to envision a fat profit from breeding your little dog, but the reality is far different.

If you love your dog—and the breed—your Shih Tzu will rack up a lot of pre-pregnancy and pregnancy-related medical

bills. First, there's testing for genetically related diseases. You don't want to pass on genetically linked health problems to a litter of puppies, so your dog should be screened for Progressive Retinal Atrophy (PRA), and you should register the results with the Canine Eye Registry Foundation (CERF). Your dog should be x-rayed for hip dysplasia (Shih Tzu have a surprisingly high rate of dysplasia for a small breed) and have her kneecaps checked (for patellar luxation), and you should register those results with the Orthopedic Foundation for Animals (OFA). You'll also want to do blood tests to check for detectible kidney disease, thyroid problems, and von Willebrand's disease. Then there's the cost of a stud fee.

Surgery Checklist

Almost every dog goes under anesthesia several times—at least to be altered and for an occasional teeth cleaning. Be sure to:

- **Ask for pre-anesthetic blood screening.** This routine blood test screens for common problems such as liver and kidney disease to make sure your dog isn't at high risk for developing surgical complications. Many veterinarians require pre-anesthetic blood work if your dog is over 7 years of age, but you should insist on it no matter what the age of your Shih Tzu. It's not very expensive, and it can prevent serious problems while your dog is under anesthesia.
- **Select a veterinarian who has the latest monitoring equipment to use during surgery.** Your dog faces the same risks during surgery as a human. Like a human, he needs to have his vital functions monitored, including his heart.
- **Ask for pain medication.** Your animal feels pain and deserves modern pain medications to make him feel more comfortable after surgery. Studies have shown that dogs (and people) who receive pain medications recover more quickly than do those who don't. Talk with your veterinarian about the best type and dose of pain medication for your pet, and be sure to follow the dosage instructions.

Your girl needs medical oversight during her pregnancy, and that means veterinary visits and sometimes ultrasounds or blood tests. Caesarean sections are fairly common in Shih Tzu, which cost more money and is an obvious health risk. Also, Shih Tzu, like other small dogs, have small litters. Your girl is likely to produce only two or three puppies.

Add it all up and, if you're a responsible breeder who does everything right for the benefit of the next generation of Shih Tzu, you will often lose money on your litters and seldom make a profit.

Emotional Costs

An emotional cost is involved in breeding. Sadly, not all puppies make it. The emotional toll of losing a puppy is considerable.

Your puppy should rebound quickly from being altered if you follow your vet's advice.

Sometimes, people have a litter so that their children can see the birth process, and then have to deal with their children's grief at the loss of some or all of a litter. (A better lesson than teaching your child about birth is to teach your child about compassion and responsibility by volunteering to help homeless or sick animals.)

Research Requirements

Responsible breeding takes knowledge and study. The future of this ancient breed lies in the hands of the people who breed them today. If you want to breed Shih Tzu, then join the American Shih Tzu Club and learn about the breed. Read the dozens of books about good breeding practices. Find mentors in the breed so that you can benefit from the experience of people who know the breed well.

PARASITES

You aren't the only one who loves your Shih Tzu. So does a whole world of parasites! Keep an eye out for signs of these creatures. Left untreated, infestations of some kinds of parasites can kill your dog.

Internal Parasites

Internal parasites are common in puppies and sometimes even in older dogs. Talk with your veterinarian if your Shih Tzu has:

- A potbelly on an otherwise thin dog
- Diarrhea
- Blood in stools
- Dull coat
- Lack of energy, listlessness
- Visible worms in feces or vomit

The first step to solving a parasite infestation is noticing that your dog has signs of worms. If you suspect your Shih Tzu has worms, don't be embarrassed. Do bring a stool sample to your veterinarian to get a diagnosis. (During your dog's annual visit to the veterinarian, you should also bring a stool sample to check for worms, even if you see no symptoms.)

Don't be tempted when you see over-the-counter medications for worms. The modern medications your veterinarian prescribes are much easier on your dog's system and safer than most of what you can find in stores.

All worms have a life cycle, and reinfestation is always possible. Don't neglect to follow through on the full course of treatment that your veterinarian recommends. Your vet will

Puppies can acquire worms from their mothers. When these worms are detected, they can be cured safely and quickly.

probably ask you to keep bringing in stool samples for a while after your dog has been cleared of worms. To keep your little dog safe, follow to the letter exactly what your veterinarian asks you to do.

Here are the major internal parasites that you and your Shih Tzu might encounter:

Roundworms

Puppies are frequently born with roundworms, even if their mothers had no sign of the parasite. Roundworms live in a dormant state in a dog's muscles. When a female becomes pregnant, hormones can cause the dormant roundworm larvae to migrate from her muscles into her milk supply and into her puppies.

Although most cases of roundworm aren't life threatening, a heavy infestation can cause vomiting, diarrhea, and even death. When you take your puppy to the veterinarian for routine vaccines and other visits, bring a stool sample so that your veterinarian can check for roundworms.

Hookworms and Whipworms

When your puppy (or adult) Shih Tzu plays in a park or goes for a walk (even in the nicest neighborhoods), he can pick up hookworms. An infected mother can also pass these parasites to her puppies. These worms are bloodsuckers that live in your dog's intestines. Left untreated, a hookworm can kill a little Shih Tzu puppy in a matter of a few weeks.

Whipworms are picked up in the environment. (A whipworm egg can live in the soil for years.) If your dog sniffs at the feces of an infected dog, or if he munches on something in infected soil, he can pick up a whipworm. Like hookworms, whipworms live in your dog's intestines. Although whipworms are unlikely to kill a mature dog, they can cause serious inflammation of the intestinal lining and cause colitis and other intestinal problems. A sign of whipworms is diarrhea with blood or mucus.

Both hookworms and whipworms respond well to medication that your veterinarian can prescribe. Over-the-counter worm medications won't treat these nasty worms. You need to ask your veterinarian for an appropriate, safe treatment.

Giving Medicine

Sooner or later, your Shih Tzu may need to take medicine. This doesn't have to be a struggle. First, try putting the medicine in your dog's food. This works if the pill doesn't have a bitter taste and if your dog is a good eater. However, some Shih Tzu taste every morsel of food and will spit the pill out. Worse yet, a sick dog may become suspicious of his food and refuse to eat—a big problem for a sick dog.

If you have a finicky Shih Tzu or are giving your dog large or bitter-tasting pills, teach your dog the word "medicine." Show your dog a yummy treat. Then say "Medicine," and quickly and efficiently give him the pill or liquid medication. Even if he squirms and wiggles, tell him "Good medicine!" and instantly give the treat. He'll soon learn to take the medicine calmly, because it always ends with something wonderful to eat.

Ask your veterinarian for medicine that's easy to swallow. Your Shih Tzu has a small mouth, and it can be hard for him to swallow a big pill. If you're having trouble, ask your veterinarian if there is a liquid form of the medication or a pill form that's easier to swallow.

Dogs who spend time outdoors in areas that may be infested are susceptible to a host of internal and external parasites.

Tapeworms

The life of a tapeworm is amazingly complex. A flea swallows blood from an infected dog and carries the tapeworm larvae to the next dog. When the next dog swallows the flea, he becomes infected with tapeworms. The creature attaches itself to the dog's intestines and robs him of his nutrition. In an extreme case, if left untreated, your dog could starve to death. Fortunately, tapeworms are easy to notice. (You can see segments of worm that look like grains of rice in the dog's feces.) They are also easily and effectively treated with a prescription from your veterinarian.

Heartworms

When your dog gets a mosquito bite, he can become infected with heartworms. These ugly worms, which look a little bit like spaghetti, live in a dog's heart and lungs. While other internal parasites usually aren't fatal to an adult dog, heartworms almost always are. They block the flow of blood to parts of a dog's lungs, which forces the heart to work harder. Eventually, the dog develops congestive heart failure. Symptoms include a loss of energy, a cough, a heart murmur, difficulty breathing, and eventual collapse.

Years ago, heartworms were a problem for dogs in the southeastern part of the United States. Now the problem has spread to virtually all corners of the country, so it is important for your Shih Tzu to be on a heartworm prevention medication. The preventive medications have low dangers of side effects in Shih Tzu. Be sure you get the appropriate dose for the size of your dog. Some heartworm preventives also help prevent infestations of whipworms and roundworms.

Don't wait until your Shih Tzu has become infected to treat him. The treatment for a heartworm infestation is dangerous and difficult, so the best defense against these horrible parasites is your dog's monthly heartworm preventive.

External Parasites

Your dog can not only get internal parasites, but he can get external parasites as well. Fortunately, safe and effective control of fleas and ticks is much easier than it used to be.

Fleas

Fleas are tiny bugs that suck your Shih Tzu's blood. If your Shih Tzu starts biting at his skin, there's a good chance he has fleas. If your Shih Tzu has a dark coat, you might not even be able to spot any fleas. If you run a wet paper towel on his coat, you might see bits of blood, because flea "dirt" (flea feces) is comprised primarily of dried blood. Another way to determine if your Shih Tzu has fleas is to put him on a white sheet and

If your Shih Tzu seems unusually lethargic or depressed, consult your vet.

Regular baths expose any fleas or ticks lurking on your dog.

comb him. You may see the dark flea "dirt" fall onto the sheet.

Fleas are so common that people don't realize they can become a major health hazard. A bad flea infestation can kill a puppy—he will lose too much blood to survive. Even a single flea can carry tapeworms and can cause allergies in your little guy. Plus, fleas just make life miserable for your dog.

If you really keep a sharp eye on your dog, you may be able to spot the problem when he only has one or two fleas. If you catch the problem right at the beginning, you may be able to solve it without resorting to chemicals. Just bathe him thoroughly, being sure to thoroughly wet and soap every square millimeter of his body. Get all the hidden places, like between his toes and under his armpits. After his bath, keep a close eye on him. You may have been lucky.

Chances are, a bath alone won't do it. If it doesn't, go to your veterinarian right away to get a prescription for one of the modern flea-killing agents. These have very low toxicity and come in doses appropriate for toy-sized dogs.

Don't buy over-the-counter flea remedies for your dog. Lots of over-the-counter products are highly toxic and will do more harm than the fleas. Better options are available at your veterinarian's office. For the health of your dog, select those products that your veterinarian recommends.

Ticks

Like fleas, ticks live by sucking your Shih Tzu's blood. Ticks look very different before and after a meal. Before they eat, they are small; some aren't much bigger than a flea. After feeding on your dog's blood, they swell to several times their original size.

Ticks frequently carry deadly diseases, including Lyme disease and Rocky Mountain spotted fever, as well as a condition called "tick paralysis," which causes paralysis and

The best flea and tick preventive is regular attention to your dog, checking all the way down to his skin.

death in dogs. In areas with heavy tick infestations, it may be a good idea to talk with your veterinarian about having your dog vaccinated against Lyme disease.

It's important to check every inch (cm) of your Shih Tzu's body after you've been out walking in grassy or wooded areas, especially if the area is known to have a lot of ticks.

When searching for ticks, pay special attention to your Shih Tzu's head, ears, neck, and toes. Also take a good look at places where body parts come together, like elbows.

Unless you have a dog who spends all his time in the city, the best idea is to prevent ticks from staying on your dog. Some of the monthly prescriptions that prevent flea infestations can also keep your dog free of ticks. Talk with your veterinarian about preventive products, especially if you like to take walks in wooded areas or if you live in a part of the country with a high incidence of tick-borne diseases.

Take immediate action if you see a tick on your Shih Tzu. Ticks bury their heads in your dog's skin. Using a pair of tweezers, clamp down as close to the head of the tick as you can, and pull out straight. Try to keep the tick intact. If you leave the head in your dog's body, take the dog to a veterinarian as soon as possible. Keep the tick's body, even if you don't go to the veterinarian, in case your dog later develops symptoms of a tick-borne disease. It can sometimes be helpful to your

Common Shih Tzu Diseases

Shih Tzu are prone to the following conditions:

- anemia
- eye problems
- hip dysplasia
- kidney disease
- thyroid disorders
- von Willebrand's disease

veterinarian to know what kind of tick bit your Shih Tzu.

Ticks can carry bacteria, so after you've removed it, wash your dog thoroughly with soap, and apply antibacterial ointment. Also, wash your own hands very thoroughly, because many tick-borne diseases affect humans as well as dogs. If you are near a veterinarian's office when you discover the tick, the best option might be to let them deal with the bug.

Getting rid of the tick is only the first step. Watch your dog for signs of tick-borne illness for the next couple of weeks. If your dog develops a fever, vomits, is wobbly on his feet, is lethargic, or shows other symptoms, take him to your veterinarian right away.

BREED-SPECIFIC HEALTH ISSUES

Every breed of dog has some health problems.

In humans, certain families are more likely to develop certain diseases. For example, some families have a tendency toward cancer, others toward heart disease. Some have more than their fair share of tooth decay, while others develop joint problems. The same is true for dogs.

Shih Tzu are generally a healthy and long-lived breed. Still, like all other purebred dogs, health issues have been identified as occurring more frequently in Shih Tzu than in most other dogs. The more you know about the health concerns in the breed, the better you can protect your little dog.

One important note: It is impossible to diagnose a disease from reading a book. If you have any concerns about your Shih Tzu's health, make an appointment with your veterinarian as soon as possible. Good health care with a great vet is your dog's ticket to a healthy, happy, long life. Regular annual physicals can also catch a disease before it shows symptoms—and that usually offers the best hope for successful treatment.

All the conditions listed below also occur in other breeds, but Shih Tzu suffer from them at a higher rate than do many other breeds, so they bear special attention.

Anemia

Some Shih Tzu develop a form of anemia called autoimmune hemolytic anemia, a condition in which the body attacks its own red blood cells.

Beautiful as they are, the position and prominence of your Shih Tzu's eyes make them prone to dirt and disease.

Symptoms

If your dog is weak, lethargic, and has an increased heart and respiration rate, these are clinical signs that he might have this disease.

Treatment

This is a serious and chronic disease. Some dogs respond well to immune-suppressing drugs, such as prednisone, and live a long, full life.

Eye Problems

Shih Tzu are prone to several genetic eye diseases. The Shih Tzu has large, prominent eyes, and his shortened nose causes the optic nerves to have an odd location, which makes the eyes far less sensitive. Also, the structure of the Shih Tzu face can lead to eye ruptures or eyes that actually leave the sockets. These are, of course, medical emergencies.

Other eye problems in the breed include progressive retinal atrophy (which causes blindness), cataracts, and various malformations of the eye that can cause the eyelashes to scar the cornea. Shih Tzu sometimes suffer from dry eye, which can usually be controlled by prescription eye drops.

Pay careful attention to your dog's eyes, and take him to the veterinarian for a checkup at any sign of discomfort.

Symptoms

If your dog is pawing at his eyes, if there is discharge around his eyes, or if he pulls away from you when your hands are near his face, you should take him to the veterinarian to have his eyes checked. If he doesn't seem to see well, it's also a time for a visit to the vet.

Treatment

The range of treatment for dog eye problems is just as diverse as it is for humans. In complex cases, your veterinarian may recommend that you see a veterinary ophthalmologist who specializes in treating eye problems in dogs and other pets.

All breeding stock should have an annual Canine Eye Registry Foundation (CERF) exam, which screens for abnormalities in the eye.

Hip Dysplasia

Hip dysplasia is the abnormal formation of the hip joint. It was a shock when breeders started x-raying Shih Tzu for hip dysplasia, because it had been assumed that this was a defect that affected large dogs, not toy dogs. However, almost 20 percent of the Shih Tzu who have been tested have been found to suffer from hip dysplasia. The good news is that, because of their small size, Shih Tzu aren't nearly as disabled by dysplasia as are large breeds.

Symptoms

A certain number of Shih Tzu tend to be snappish when touched or groomed. More than likely, these dogs are in pain from this condition.

Treatment

All Shih Tzu should have their hips x-rayed before they are bred. No dog with poor hips should be part of the Shih Tzu gene pool, no matter how nearly perfect he is otherwise.

Dogs with this condition can receive pain medication, acupuncture, or chiropractic treatments to ease the discomfort. In serious cases, surgery is also an option.

Kidney Disease

Shih Tzu sometimes suffer from renal dysplasia—a form of kidney disease in which the kidneys never develop properly in a puppy. The disease is eventually fatal. All breeding stock should be screened for kidney function, but unfortunately, abnormal kidney function levels sometimes don't appear until the dog is old enough to have been bred. Because of this, the American Shih Tzu Club, along with the AKC and other advocates, are funding research to find a genetic marker to help determine which dogs carry the genetic predisposition for this disease.

Learning which diseases your Shih Tzu is prone to helps you be alert to their symptoms.

Symptoms

There are no symptoms in the early stage of this chronic disease. After a significant amount of kidney damage has occurred, dogs develop excessive thirst, produce excessive amounts of urine, and suffer from weight loss and lack of vigor. In the later stage of the disease, blood tests show reduced kidney function as well.

Treatment

Some dogs can live a full life span with the disease, while others have their lives cut tragically short. No special treatment is available for the disease, but a low-protein diet may help keep a dog feeling better.

Thyroid Disorders

The thyroids are small glands that have a lot to do with controlling your dog's metabolism. Thyroid disorders are somewhat common in Shih Tzu, and the best breeders have their breeding stock tested for thyroid problems.

Symptoms

Common symptoms of thyroid problems are weight gain, lethargy, and poor coat (sometimes including hair loss). Your veterinarian will perform a simple blood test to make a definitive diagnosis.

Treatment

Happily, thyroid problems are not life threatening and are effectively treated with medication.

Von Willebrand's Disease

In von Willebrand's disease, the blood doesn't clot properly. It's a common inherited disorder in several breeds, including Shih Tzu. Dogs should be tested before breeding to ensure that they don't have the disease.

Symptoms

Your dog may have the disease without any obvious symptoms. However, some dogs with von Willebrand's disease may show signs of abnormal bleeding from the gums, bloody urine, nose bleeds, or intestinal bleeding. Your veterinarian can perform certain tests to determine if your Shih Tzu has this disease.

Treatment

If your dog has been identified as having von Willebrand's disease, your veterinarian will take extra precautions during surgical procedures and may have special transfusion medications available in case of an emergency.

HEALTH PROBLEMS COMMON IN SMALL DOGS

Because of their small size, toy dogs have several conditions every Shih Tzu owner should be on the lookout for. They include the following.

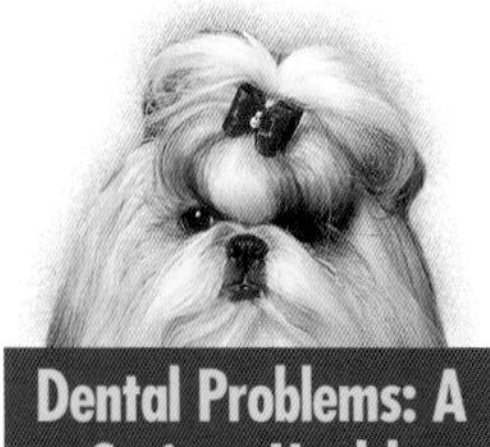

Dental Problems: A Serious Health Concern

Dental problems are a lot more serious than just "dog breath" or even lost teeth. Bacteria in your dog's mouth can circulate throughout his body and can lead to heart, liver, and kidney disease, among other serious health concerns.

Broken Bones

Although Shih Tzu are sturdier than most toy dogs, they can still break a bone fairly easily, whether they're youngsters or adults. Don't let your Shih Tzu fling himself off tables or off the back of the couch, especially when he's a puppy. Be careful when you pick him up—hold him carefully so that he doesn't wriggle loose and fall.

Symptoms

If your dog is limping and reluctant to put weight on his leg, especially after a fall, take him to your veterinarian right away. This could be a medical emergency.

Treatment

Watch your puppy at all times, and seek first-rate medical attention immediately if he's in pain after a fall. If your puppy breaks a bone, your veterinarian will give him very much the same kind of care your doctor would give you. The injury will be x-rayed. Depending on the kind of break and what bone has been broken, treatment may consist of simple rest, soft or hard casts, or surgery.

Because Shih Tzu are prone to dental problems, proper care must begin during puppyhood.

Dental Problems

Dental problems are common in all small breeds, and Shih Tzu have some of the worst problems, even among toy breeds.

If you think about it for a moment, it makes sense. Dogs' teeth are basically designed to fit in a wolf's mouth. Compared to a wolf, a Shih Tzu's mouth is both small and oddly shaped. Your dog's short face changes the way his teeth are aligned, so the teeth don't scrape against each other like those of a larger, long-muzzled dog.

Toy-dog dental problems have a larger margin for error than do the dental problems of larger dogs. A millimeter pocket in the gum of a Labrador Retriever (or even a human) is a small problem. A millimeter pocket in your Shih Tzu's little mouth might lead to the loss of a tooth.

It is not unusual for Shih Tzu puppies to need one or more of their puppy teeth extracted. Puppy teeth normally fall out when a dog is about 6 months old, to be replaced by permanent, adult teeth. However, small dogs tend to retain one or more puppy teeth, and Shih Tzu are no exception. A retained puppy tooth can cause adult teeth to become crooked and add to dental problems in the long-term. If your puppy still has one or more puppy teeth by the time he's about 7 or 8 months old, your

With their short noses and thick coats, Shih Tzu are quite sensitive to heat.

veterinarian will probably recommend that you have the tooth removed. Some people wait until their puppy is altered to have any remaining puppy teeth extracted, so the puppy only has to go under general anesthesia once.

Preventive Care

The best way to keep your Shih Tzu's teeth healthy is to brush them every day. Dogs can't floss, but playing with stuffed toys helps to scrub away tartar. Although a stuffed toy won't remove serious tartar buildup, the scrubbing action of playing tug-of-war and chewing on a toy provides a certain amount of "brushing" action. You'll both have fun, and you'll be improving his dental health while you play.

Healthy chew toys help keep your Shih Tzu's teeth clean and his mouth healthy. Raw bones can be a good dental cleaner, as long as the bones are large enough not to get lodged in your dog's throat. Of course, only let your little buddy chew bones when you're there to supervise. Do not ever give your dog a cooked bone. A cooked bone will splinter and can cause internal bleeding.

What food your Shih Tzu eats can also make a difference in preventing dental disease. People who advocate feeding raw diets say the enzymes in raw food help keep a dog's teeth clean. If you're thinking about feeding your dog a raw food diet, this is certainly a benefit to consider. Otherwise, be sure your dog eats dry kibble, which can provide scrubbing action on his teeth. Canned food is the worst choice from a dental perspective—it's mushy and tends to stick to a dog's teeth, which makes tartar accumulate more rapidly.

Professional Dental Care

One of the most important parts of your dog's annual physical exam is his dental checkup. Your veterinarian will check for the build-up of tartar on your Shih Tzu's teeth and look for teeth that aren't healthy. If your dog has dental disease, don't delay treatment. It will only make the problem worse.

Hypoglycemia

Hypoglycemia, or low blood sugar, occurs fairly frequently in toy-breed puppies. It's most common when puppies are between 6 and 12 weeks old. (This is another reason to purchase toy dogs over the age of 12 weeks.) A hypoglycemic episode is most likely to happen if your Shih Tzu is feeling stressed, has skipped a meal or has a poor diet, is cold, or has used up too much energy playing too long at one time.

Heat and Shih Tzu

Combine a short-nosed dog and long hair, and you have an animal who is very sensitive to heat. Be careful not to let your Shih Tzu get too hot. If he becomes distressed, pour cool (not ice cold) water on him. If he seems disoriented, wobbly, or weak, take him to the veterinarian after you have cooled him down.

Symptoms

You might notice your dog staggering, seeming depressed or lethargic, or acting disoriented. The condition can also cause your dog to slip into a coma and die.

Treatment

If your dog is showing signs of hypoglycemia, rub Karo syrup or honey on his gums, or mix a little bit of the syrup or honey in some water and place it on his tongue. Meanwhile, call your veterinarian right away for instructions for further treatment. Repeated episodes can lead to further, more severe complications, so work with your veterinarian to manage this problem.

Shih Tzu puppies typically eat four meals a day until they are 12 weeks old, then three meals until they are 6 months old, and two meals during their adult years. If you have a dog who is prone to hypoglycemia, talk with your veterinarian about giving your Shih Tzu more frequent, small meals to keep his blood sugar levels more even.

Dogs with this condition usually outgrow it by the time they're 7 months old.

Liver Shunts

Occasionally, the liver doesn't form correctly before a puppy is born. When your puppy is still in his mother's uterus, a vein carries his blood past his liver, because the mother dog's system is already filtering the puppy's bloodstream. Normally, this vein

Puppies between 6 and 12 weeks of age can be hypoglycemic, a condition they usually outgrow by 7 months of age.

seals itself off, and the puppy's liver assumes this job after birth.

Sometimes, unfortunately, the vein remains intact, so the puppy's bloodstream bypasses the cleansing functions of the liver. As a result, waste products build up inside your puppy's system. Plus, the liver can't do its job of storing nutrients, so dogs with liver shunts don't properly thrive and grow.

Symptoms

Dogs with liver shunts often have digestive troubles, such as chronic diarrhea, and may also be unusually thirsty. They commonly have serious neurological problems. Small size and failure to gain weight are very common in puppies with liver shunts.

Treatment

If the disease isn't too severe, it can be managed with medications and a low-protein diet. Some cases are best treated with surgery to close the shunt.

Luxating Patella

A slipping kneecap, called a luxating patella, is a common problem in all toy-sized breeds (and some larger ones). The kneecap in your dog's rear leg is attached by a groove in the bone. A toy dog's smaller bones make it easier for the kneecap to pop out of the groove.

Luxating patellas range from a painless "trick knee" that requires no medical attention to severe cases that required skilled surgery. The condition is rated on a scale of 1 to 4, with 1 being a patella that can be pushed out of place but isn't painful and readily goes back into place, and 4 being a patella that is always out of place and very painful. Surgery is usually recommended for grades 3 and 4.

Symptoms

Many dogs with luxating patellas have a distinctive hop or skip. It may seem cute, until you realize that it's a sign of a serious medical condition.

Treatment

Luxating patella surgery isn't cheap, because it is usually performed by an orthopedic surgeon. Because there's reason to believe that a tendency toward luxating patellas is hereditary, buy your puppy from a breeder who has her dogs checked for luxating patellas.

Human Medicines and Dogs

Pain medication that is safe and effective for humans can be deadly for dogs. One regular-strength (200 mg) ibuprofen tablet can cause stomach ulcers in a 10-pound (4.5-kg) dog. Do not give your Shih Tzu aspirin or any other pain reliever without discussing it with your veterinarian first!

DISEASES OF OLD AGE

Happily, most Shih Tzu live well into their senior years. Of course, you want those years to be happy, comfortable, and healthy for your old guy. Some common diseases face all senior dogs, including Shih Tzu, but with today's medical advances, your Shih Tzu can be treated and live well, even if he develops these typical aging problems.

Arthritis

Shih Tzu have a high rate of hip dysplasia for a small breed and are a bit more likely to develop arthritis in their old age than are most other small dogs.

Symptoms

If you notice that your dog is stiff and sore, especially as he ages, talk with your veterinarian.

Treatment

Your veterinarian may prescribe anti-inflammatory medication or supplements, such as glucosamine or chondroitin sulphate. Alternative treatments, such as acupuncture, physical therapy, and chiropractic therapy, can also bring a lot of comfort to a dog with arthritis or other chronic pain.

Cancer

Cancer is the leading cause of death among senior dogs. Effective treatments are available for many cancers that can prolong your dog's life for years.

Like all dogs, senior Shih Tzu are affected by the ailments of old age. Your extra care and attention are critical through his golden years.

Symptoms

The best defense against cancer is early detection, so watch your Shih Tzu for lumps and bumps on his skin. Cancer can often have subtle symptoms, so if your dog is lethargic or doesn't seem to be his regular self, don't hesitate to take him to the veterinarian.

Treatment

Cancer treatments include surgery, chemotherapy, and radiation. Some animal hospitals in larger cities even have full-time cancer specialists.

Cancer treatments for dogs are much less invasive than human treatments, so explore your options before making a decision. Radiation treatments can sometimes cause temporary burning of the skin. In almost all cases, the doses of chemotherapy given to dogs are too small to cause hair loss.

Canine Cognitive Dysfunction

This disease is much like Alzheimer's disease in people.

Symptoms

Some of the symptoms include pacing, panting, getting lost in a corner of the house, and loss of potty training. Some dogs suffer from personality changes, even becoming aggressive toward people they love.

Treatment

Dogs who get a lot of mental and physical exercise are less likely to develop the disease than are "couch potatoes"—another good reason to play games with your Shih Tzu and keep up those walks!

If your Shih Tzu develops canine cognitive dysfunction, don't despair. Your veterinarian can prescribe medications that may significantly help your dog.

Heart Disease

Older dogs, like older humans, frequently develop heart disease.

Symptoms

The most common signs of heart disease are intolerance to exercise and coughing.

Treatment

Your Shih Tzu has the same range of options for treatment that you do—all the way from managing symptoms with medications, such as diuretics, to open heart surgery or pacemakers. Your veterinarian might refer you to a veterinary cardiologist who has the same kinds of equipment as does a cardiologist for humans.

Know the Way!

In most larger cities, and many smaller ones, after-hours emergencies are handled at special emergency clinics. Take the time now to familiarize yourself with how to get there, so you know the fastest route to take if your Shih Tzu becomes sick.

Incontinence

Older dogs often forget their housetraining. Often, this is a sign of canine cognitive dysfunction, and treating the disease will solve the problem. At other times, incontinence can be a sign of bladder problems. Older female dogs, especially, can begin to have trouble controlling their bladders.

Symptoms

Symptoms include losing control of bladder or bowel functions, whether your dog is awake or asleep.

Treatment

Medication is very effective in treating this problem. Remember, your older Shih Tzu doesn't mean to lose his housetraining knowledge. Be kind, gentle, and compassionate if he's having some problems.

MEDICAL EMERGENCIES

Be ready for medical emergencies by having a first-aid kit ready. You can purchase a pet first-aid kit at pet supply stores or over the Internet, or you can put one together yourself.

Here's what you should have in your kit:

- Antibiotic ointment
- Antihistamine (in case of bee sting or similar incident—ask

Dealing With a Terminal Illness

When you hear that your dog has a terminal illness, you may think you need to euthanize him right away. That isn't necessarily the case, though. With today's modern pain medications (and alternative treatments, such as acupuncture), many pets can live comfortably for weeks, months, or even years with chronic conditions that would otherwise be intolerable.

Even if your dog has an illness that has a very short-term prognosis, you can use pain management to give both of you extra time together. It can allow you to take a few hours or days to say goodbye. It can even allow you time to decide how and when to let your dog go.

your veterinarian about the correct dosage for your Shih Tzu, and keep this information with your kit)

- Hot/cold pack
- Muzzle (or strip of soft cloth to make into a muzzle)
- Nonstick gauze pads
- Pet first-aid book (read through the book ahead of time so you know where to turn when a real emergency happens)
- Phone number and address of the nearest emergency veterinary clinic
- Phone number for your veterinarian (you don't want to be fumbling through the phone book in an emergency)
- Scissors
- "Space" blanket that insulates against heat and cold
- Syringe (no needle attached) to administer medicine or liquids
- Towels to wrap your dog in if he is cold or in shock, and to help clean dirt or blood
- Tweezers
- Vet wrap (bandaging that sticks to itself)

Determining a Medical Emergency

Call your veterinarian immediately if your Shih Tzu:

- Can't move his legs
- Has a seizure
- Has an eye injury
- Has been hit by a car, even if he seems okay
- Has blood in his urine or feces
- Has difficulty breathing
- Has persistent, repeated vomiting—or persistently tries to vomit
- Is acutely lethargic (can't move or stand up, or seems unaware of his surroundings)
- Is bleeding
- Strains to potty

PAYING FOR MEDICAL CARE

The great strides in modern medical care for dogs often don't come cheaply. Think now about how you're going to deal with medical costs for your Shih Tzu to prevent unpleasant surprises later.

Plan ahead to determine how you will care for your dog in an emergency.

Health Insurance for Pets

One option is health insurance for dogs. This can be a good option for Shih Tzu owners, especially because some health problems in the breed (such as kidney disease) can be expensive to treat.

Several pet health insurance companies have come and gone quickly in the last few years, so look for a company that's been in business for a long time. Don't worry about routine care coverage—that isn't what adds up to excessive health care costs. When you're comparing companies' coverages, run through an example of an acute condition (such as surgery for an accident) and a chronic one (such as a medical condition that requires a sizable amount of monthly medical expenses).

Thousands of employers now offer pet health insurance as a company benefit. If your employer offers it, use it! If your employer doesn't offer it, find out if they'd be willing to consider adding it to their benefit package.

There are alternatives to pet insurance. Some veterinary clinics offer access to a company that provides loans to people who have pet health care costs they can't afford to pay. You also might keep a credit card open with a high limit, just in case your dog needs it.

Think about how you'll pay now, so cost won't be part of the difficult decision-making you'll have to face if your Shih Tzu becomes seriously sick or injured.

ALTERNATIVE CARE

Many kinds of alternative health care are now part of the mainstream for humans. The same kinds of alternative treatments that you might use, such as acupuncture, chiropractic treatments, herbs, and homeopathy, are available for your Shih Tzu. These treatments are becoming more popular by the year and are often worth exploring.

Alternative and Western medicine aren't necessarily mutually exclusive. You would certainly take your dog to a conventional veterinarian if he broke a bone, but you might also consult a homeopath for treatments that promote healing, or a massage therapist to help make your dog feel better.

If you're the kind of person who goes to an acupuncturist or naturopathic doctor, or if conventional medication isn't working for your Shih Tzu, you may want to try alternative medicine for your dog. Many veterinarians specialize in alternative treatments. A good place to find a referral for a holistic veterinarian is the American Holistic Veterinary Association (www.ahvma.org). This association's website has a good discussion of alternative therapies and has a listing of members by state.

Acupuncture

If you have a needle phobia, don't panic. Acupuncture needles aren't painful for humans or dogs. Unlike hypodermic needles, which are designed to pierce tissue to deliver a shot, the hair-thin acupuncture needles go between layers of skin. Acupuncture can help reduce pain and is often effective in treating allergies and other health problems.

To find an acupuncturist, check out the International Veterinary Acupuncture Society (www.ivas.org). This professional association provides training and certification for veterinarians who want to practice acupuncture. Their website includes a listing of certified members. (You may also consider checking with a human acupuncturist in your area if your state medical and veterinary laws allow acupuncturists to treat animals.)

For both preventive and curative care, alternative treatments can aid in the overall wellness of your dog.

Chinese Herbs

Chinese herbal medicine has been practiced for thousands of years. Herbs can be just as potent as Western medicines, so be sure to work with a knowledgeable practitioner who knows if the herb has side effects or doesn't mix well with other medications your dog may be taking.

Chiropractic Treatments

Chiropractic treatments realign your dog's skeletal system to put it back in healthy, functioning order. This can be especially helpful after injuries and accidents, or for dogs with chronic problems, such as arthritis. The American Veterinary Chiropractic Association (www.animalchiropractic.org) provides training and certification for chiropractors and veterinarians. This association has certified practitioners listed on their website, which are split fairly evenly between veterinarians and chiropractors. Members are in the United States, Canada, Europe, and Australia.

Homeopathy

Holistic veterinarians are likely to use homeopathic medications and herbs, both of which are different from conventional Western medicines. Homeopathy was developed in the 1800s and is based on the concept that "like cures like."

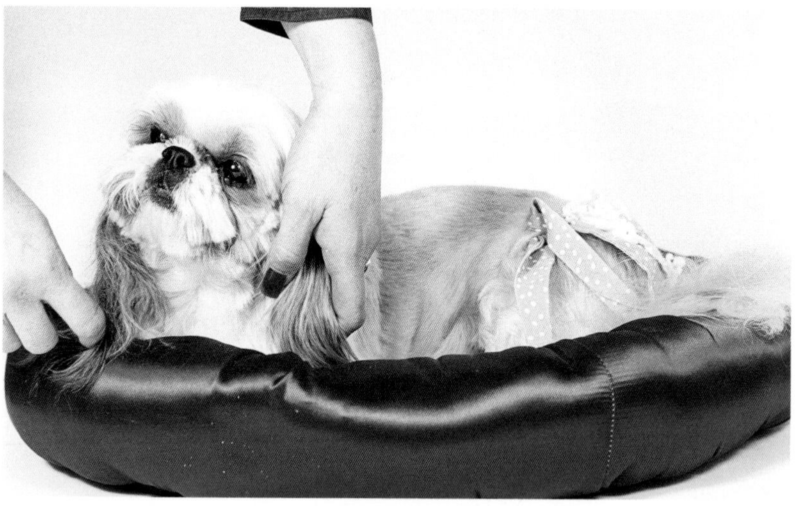

You can turn regular petting into a soothing and healing massage for your dog with just a few well-mastered strokes.

Much like a vaccine teaches the body to have an immune response to a disease by introducing a debilitated virus, homeopathy is designed to help the body overcome an illness by introducing a small dose of a substance that, in larger doses, would cause the symptoms the practitioner is trying to cure. In short, a tiny dose will cure, while a larger dose will make the body sick. Because homeopathic treatments contain only tiny amounts of active substances, they generally don't impact the effectiveness of conventional medication.

Tellington Touch (TTouch)

Linda Tellington-Jones developed a system of feather-like touches (TTouch) that quickly became a popular form of healing. TTouch relaxes and calms a dog and can help you establish a closer rapport with your pet. It gives your pet a sense of wellbeing and may help him feel better if he's sick. Many TTouch practitioners teach classes, so you can learn to TTouch your own dog. Several books and videos are available, many of which are carried at local libraries. To learn more about TTouch, go to Linda Tellington-Jones' website (www.tteam-ttouch.com). It gives a listing of TTouch practitioners around the world.

SAYING GOODBYE

The hardest part of loving an animal is knowing that someday you will have to say goodbye. The final gift you can give to your Shih Tzu is to help him leave this world gently.

Even a sick dog can continue to have a good life if properly cared for.

Many people struggle hugely with the decision of when it's time to euthanize a terminally ill pet. The answer lies within your heart—and with your dog. No one knows your dog as well as you do, and he will let you know when he's ready to go. There are countless stories of people whose dogs gave them what seem to be tangible signs of saying goodbye. A dog will pick up a toy he hasn't played with since he was a puppy and bring it to you, or he will go up to each member of the household with a special greeting. You can feel it when a dog has closed the circle of his life.

More likely, you will see the readiness in your dog's sweet eyes. He's lost his zest for life, his body hurts all the time, and he isn't interested in eating any more. Some dogs die naturally in their sleep. In most cases, however, they are ready to go before their bodies give out entirely, and it is a kind and loving act to end their suffering.

Euthanasia—A Gentle Procedure

When your veterinarian euthanizes your pet, it is a painless, gentle procedure. Your veterinarian will simply give your dog a shot with an overdose of anesthetic. Your dog will softly fall into unconsciousness. When he is fully under the anesthesia, his heart will simply stop beating. It is quick and surprisingly peaceful.

It will help both you and your dog if you can be there for the procedure. When you see the peacefulness with which your dog's spirit left this world, you will be comforted. It is also nice for your dog to have your loving presence with him as he gently falls into unconsciousness.

Euthanasia at Home

Your veterinarian may be willing to come to your home, or you may want to call a veterinarian who does house calls. You can sit with your Shih Tzu on your lap or sit with him outside in the sun when you say goodbye.

You and your Shih Tzu will accumulate many special memories as you go through life together.

Whether it's a mobile veterinarian or your personal veterinarian who has cared for your dog for years, you will see the compassion and love the people in this profession have for the animals they serve.

Other Pets Also Need to Say Goodbye

Animals who share a home love each other just as much as they love their humans. It is very helpful for them to see their buddy's body and understand that he is gone. "Animals understand death, but they don't understand disappearance," one of my wisest friends once said. So, if it is possible, let your other dogs (and cats, if they were close to the dog) sniff his body. Let them understand what happened. Dogs who have seen the body of their friends are much less likely to frantically search for their missing companions.

Memorials and Rituals

Different people find different things helpful in the grieving process. There is no right or wrong answer—do what feels natural and right for you. To some people, an animal's body isn't important—they would rather not have the remains. Others find saying goodbye in a physical way helpful.

Burial

Many people find it a comfort to bury their little dog in a favorite place in the yard. Do be aware that some cities prohibit this, however.

Cremation

Cremation has become very common. You can scatter your Shih Tzu's ashes in his favorite place to play. Alternatively, you can keep the remains in an urn, perhaps decorated with your dog's collar. You can even order artwork and jewelry that will incorporate some of your dog's ashes in the art.

Memorializing Your Shih Tzu

There are countless ways to memorialize what your dog gave to you in his lifetime. Give a donation to an animal shelter or Shih Tzu rescue in your dog's name. Plant a tree. Write a poem. Do whatever brings you comfort. There is no "right" or "wrong" way to grieve the loss of a pet.

Pet Loss Support

The little dog with bright eyes and a loving heart changed your life. It is normal and healthy to grieve that loss. If you think some support would help you, ask your veterinarian if a pet loss support group is available in your area—many communities have them.

With all the love and care you're giving your Shih Tzu, he's likely to have an especially long and happy life. Use the information in this chapter to help your little dog thrive.

Shih Tzu are magical dogs. Their human-like faces, soulful eyes, and sometimes clownish ways make us all grateful to share our years with them. Just think, for as long as maybe 10,000 years, a string of people have loved and protected the ancestors of this breed. Today, it is your turn. Celebrate the joy that you and your little dog bring to each other!

Lots of love and care will help your Shih Tzu thrive.

APPENDIX

THE AMERICAN KENNEL CLUB BREED STANDARD

General Appearance:

The Shih Tzu is a sturdy, lively, alert toy dog with long flowing double coat. Befitting his noble Chinese ancestry as a highly valued, prized companion and palace pet, the Shih Tzu is proud of bearing, has a distinctively arrogant carriage with head well up and tail curved over the back. Although there has always been considerable size variation, the Shih Tzu must be compact, solid, carrying good weight and substance.

Even though a toy dog, the Shih Tzu must be subject to the same requirements of soundness and structure prescribed for all breeds, and any deviation from the ideal described in the standard should be penalized to the extent of the deviation. Structural faults common to all breeds are as undesirable in the Shih Tzu as in any other breed, regardless of whether or not such faults are specifically mentioned in the standard.

Size, Proportion, Substance:

Size—Ideally, height at withers is 9 to 10½ inches; but, not less than 8 inches nor more than 11 inches. Ideally, weight of mature dogs, 9 to 16 pounds. ***Proportion***—Length between withers and root of tail is slightly longer than height at withers. *The Shih Tzu must never be so high stationed as to appear leggy, nor so low stationed as to appear dumpy or squatty.* ***Substance***—Regardless of size, the Shih Tzu is always compact, solid and carries good weight and substance.

Head:

Head—Round, broad, wide between eyes, its size in balance with the overall size of dog being neither too large nor too small. ***Fault:*** Narrow head, close-set eyes. ***Expression***—Warm, sweet, wide-eyed, friendly and trusting. An overall well-balanced and pleasant expression supersedes the importance of individual parts. *Care should be taken to look and examine well beyond the hair to determine if what is seen is the actual head and expression rather than an image created by grooming technique.* **Eyes**—Large, round, not prominent, placed well apart, looking straight ahead. *Very dark.* Lighter on liver pigmented dogs and blue pigmented dogs. ***Fault:*** Small, close-set or light eyes; excessive eye white. ***Ears***—Large, set slightly below crown of skull; heavily coated. ***Skull***—Domed. ***Stop***—There is a *definite stop.* ***Muzzle***—Square, short, unwrinkled, with good cushioning, set no lower than bottom eye rim; never downturned. Ideally, no longer than 1 inch from tip of nose to stop, although length may vary slightly in relation to overall size of dog. Front of muzzle should be flat; lower lip and chin not protruding and definitely never receding. ***Fault:*** Snipiness, lack of definite stop. ***Nose***—Nostrils are broad, wide, and open. ***Pigmentation***—Nose, lips, eye rims are black on all colors, except liver on liver pigmented dogs and blue on blue pigmented dogs. ***Fault:*** Pink on nose, lips, or eye rims. ***Bite***—Undershot. Jaw is broad and wide. A missing tooth or slightly misaligned teeth should not be too severely penalized. Teeth and tongue should not show when mouth is closed. ***Fault:*** Overshot bite.

Neck, Topline, Body:

Of utmost importance is an overall well-balanced dog with no exaggerated features. ***Neck***—Well set-on flowing smoothly into shoulders; of sufficient length to permit natural high head carriage and in balance with height and length of dog. ***Topline***—Level. ***Body***—Short-coupled and sturdy with no waist or tuck-up. The Shih Tzu is slightly longer than tall. ***Fault:*** Legginess. ***Chest*** -Broad and deep with good spring-of-rib, however, not barrel-chested. Depth of ribcage should extend to just below elbow. Distance from elbow to withers is a little greater than from elbow to ground. ***Croup***—Flat. ***Tail***—Set on high, heavily plumed, carried in curve well over back. Too loose, too tight, too flat, or too low set a tail is undesirable and should be penalized to extent of deviation.

Forequarters:

Shoulders—Well-angulated, well laid-back, well laid-in, fitting smoothly into body. ***Legs***—Straight, well-boned, muscular, set well-apart and under chest, with elbows set close to body. ***Pasterns***—Strong, perpendicular. ***Dewclaws***—May be removed. ***Feet***—Firm, well-padded, point straight ahead.

Hindquarters:

Angulation of hindquarters should be in balance with forequarters. ***Legs***—Well-boned, muscular, and straight when viewed from rear with well-bent stifles, not close set but in line with forequarters. ***Hocks***—Well let down, perpendicular. ***Fault:*** Hyperextension of hocks. ***Dewclaws***—May be removed. ***Feet***—Firm, well-padded, point straight ahead.

Coat:

Coat—Luxurious, double-coated, dense, long, and flowing. Slight wave permissible. Hair on top of head is tied up. ***Fault:*** Sparse coat, single coat, curly coat. ***Trimming***—Feet, bottom of coat, and anus may be done for neatness and to facilitate movement. ***Fault:*** Excessive trimming.

Color and Markings:

All are permissible and to be considered *equally*.

Gait:

The Shih Tzu moves straight and must be shown at its own natural speed, *neither raced nor strung-up*, to evaluate its smooth, flowing, effortless movement with good front reach and equally strong rear drive, level topline, naturally high head carriage, and tail carried in gentle curve over back.

Temperament:

As the sole purpose of the Shih Tzu is that of a companion and house pet, it is essential that its temperament be outgoing, happy, affectionate, friendly and trusting towards all.

Approved May 9, 1989
Effective June 29, 1989

THE KENNEL CLUB BREED STANDARD

General Appearance:
Sturdy, abundantly coated dog with distinctly arrogant carriage and chrysanthemum-like face.

Characteristics:
Intelligent, active and alert.

Temperament:
Friendly and independent.

Head and Skull:
Head broad, round, wide between eyes. Shock-headed with hair falling well over eyes. Good beard and whiskers, hair growing upwards on the nose giving a distinctly chrysanthemum-like effect. Muzzle of ample width, square, short, not wrinkled; flat and hairy. Nose black but dark liver in liver or liver marked dogs and about one inch from tip to definite stop. Nose level or slightly tip-tilted. Top of nose leather should be on a line with or slightly below lower eyerim. Wide-open nostrils. Down-pointed nose highly undesirable, as are pinched nostrils. Pigmentation of muzzle as unbroken as possible.

Eyes:
Large, dark, round, placed well apart but not prominent. Warm expression. In liver or liver-marked dogs, lighter eye colour permissible. No white of eye showing.

Ears:
Large, with long leathers, carried drooping. Set slightly below crown of skull, so heavily coated they appear to blend into hair of neck.

Mouth:
Wide, slightly undershot or level. Lips level.

Neck:
Well proportioned, nicely arched. Sufficient length to carry head proudly.

Forequarters:
Shoulders well laid back. Legs short and muscular with ample bone, as straight as possible, consistent with broad chest being well let down.

Body:
Longer between withers and root of tail than height of withers, well coupled and sturdy, chest broad and deep, shoulders firm, back level.

Hindquarters:
Legs short and muscular with ample bone. Straight when viewed from the rear. Thighs well rounded and muscular. Legs looking massive on account of wealth of hair.

Feet:
Rounded, firm and well padded, appearing big on account of wealth of hair.

Tail:
Heavily plumed, carried gaily well over back. Set on high. Height approximately level with that of skull to give a balanced outline.

Gait/Movement:
Arrogant, smooth-flowing, front legs reaching well forward, strong rear action and showing full pad.

Coat:
Long, dense, not curly, with good undercoat. Slight wave permitted. Strongly recommended that hair on head tied up.

Colour:
All colours permissible, white blaze on forehead and white tip to tail highly desirable in parti-colours.

Size:
Height at withers not more than 27 cms (10½ ins), type and breed characteristics of the utmost importance and on no account to be sacrificed to size alone. Weight: 4.5-8 kgs (10-18 lbs). Ideal weight 4.5-7.5 kgs (10-16 lbs).

Faults:
Any departure from the foregoing points should be considered a fault and the seriousness with which the fault should be regarded should be in exact proportion to its degree and its effect upon the health and welfare of the dog.

Note:
Male animals should have two apparently normal testicles fully descended into the scrotum.

September 2000

ASSOCIATIONS AND ORGANIZATIONS

Breed Clubs

American Kennel Club (AKC)
5580 Centerview Drive
Raleigh, NC 27606
Telephone: (919) 233-9767
Fax: (919) 233-3627
E-mail: info@akc.org
www.akc.org

American Shih Tzu Club (ASTC)
Corresponding Secretary: Alyce A. Kotze
www.shihtzu.org

Canadian Kennel Club (CKC)
89 Skyway Avenue, Suite 100
Etobicoke, Ontario M9W 6R4
Telephone: (416) 675-5511
Fax: (416) 675-6506
E-mail: information@ckc.ca
www.ckc.ca

The Kennel Club
1 Clarges Street
London
W1J 8AB
Telephone: 0870 606 6750
Fax: 0207 518 1058
www.the-kennel-club.org.uk

United Kennel Club (UKC)
100 E. Kilgore Road
Kalamazoo, MI 49002-5584
Telephone: (269) 343-9020
Fax: (269) 343-7037
E-mail: pbickell@ukcdogs.com
www.ukcdogs.com

Rescue Organizations and Animal Welfare Groups

American Humane Association (AHA)
63 Inverness Drive East
Englewood, CO 80112
Telephone: (303) 792-9900
Fax: 792-5333
www.americanhumane.org

American Society for the Prevention of Cruelty to Animals (ASPCA)
424 E. 92nd Street
New York, NY 10128-6804
Telephone: (212) 876-7700
www.aspca.org

Royal Society for the Prevention of Cruelty to Animals (RSPCA)
Telephone: 0870 3335 999
Fax: 0870 7530 284
www.rspca.org.uk

The Humane Society of the United States (HSUS)
2100 L Street, NW
Washington DC 20037
Telephone: (202) 452-1100
www.hsus.org

Sports

Canine Freestyle Federation, Inc.
Membership Secretary: Brandy Clymire
E-mail: CFFmemberinfo@aol.com
www.canine-freestyle.org

International Agility Link (IAL)
Global Administrator: Steve Drinkwater
E-mail: yunde@powerup.au
www.agilityclick.com/~ial

North American Flyball Association (NAFA)
1400 West Devon Avenue #512
Chicago, IL 60660
Telephone: (800) 318-6312
Fax: (800) 318-6318
www.flyball.org

Veterinary Resources

Academy of Veterinary Homeopathy (AVH)
P.O. Box 9280
Wilmington, DE 19809
Telephone: (866) 652-1590
Fax: (866) 652-1590
E-mail: office@TheAVH.org
www.theavh.org

American Academy of Veterinary Acupuncture (AAVA)
100 Roscommon Drive, Suite 320
Middletown, CT 06457
Telephone: (860) 635-6300
Fax: (860) 635-6400
E-mail: office@aava.org
www.aava.org

American Animal Hospital Association (AAHA)
P.O. Box 150899
Denver, CO 80215-0899
Telephone: (303) 986-2800
Fax: (303) 986-1700
E-mail: info@aahanet.org
www.aahanet.org/index.cfm

American Holistic Veterinary Medical Association (AHVMA)
2218 Old Emmorton Road
Bel Air, MD 21015
Telephone: (410) 569-0795
Fax: (410) 569-2346
E-mail: office@ahvma.org
www.ahvma.org

American Veterinary Medical Association (AVMA)
1931 North Meacham Road – Suite 100
Schaumburg, IL 60173
Telephone: (847) 925-8070
Fax: (847) 925-1329
E-mail: avmainfo@avma.org
www.avma.org

British Veterinary Association (BVA)
7 Mansfield Street
London
W1G 9NQ
Telephone: 020 7636 6541
Fax: 020 7436 2970
E-mail: bvahq@bva.co.uk
www.bva.co.uk

Miscellaneous

Association of Pet Dog Trainers (APDT)
150 Executive Center Drive Box 35
Greenville, SC 29615
Telephone: (800) PET-DOGS
Fax: (864) 331-0767
E-mail: information@apdt.com
www.apdt.com

Delta Society
875 124th Ave NE, Suite 101
Bellevue, WA 98005
Telephone: (425) 226-7357
Fax: (425) 235-1076
E-mail: info@deltasociety.org
www.deltasociety.org

Therapy Dogs International (TDI)
88 Bartley Road
Flanders, NJ 07836
Telephone: (973) 252-9800
Fax: (973) 252-7171
E-mail: tdi@gti.net
www.tdi-dog.org

PUBLICATIONS

Books

Lane, Dick, and Neil Ewart. *A-Z of Dog Diseases & Health Problems*. New York: Howell Books, 1997.

Rubenstein, Eliza, and Shari Kalina. *The Adoption Option: Choosing and Raising the Shelter Dog for You.* New York: Howell Books, 1996.

Serpell, James. *The Domestic Dog: Its Evolution, Behaviour and Interactions with People.* Cambridge: Cambridge University Press, 1995.

Magazines

AKC Family Dog
American Kennel Club
260 Madison Avenue
New York, NY 10016
Telephone: (800) 490-5675
E-mail: familydog@akc.org
www.akc.org/pubs/familydog

AKC Gazette
American Kennel Club
260 Madison Avenue
New York, NY 10016
Telephone: (800) 533-7323
E-mail: gazette@akc.org
www.akc.org/pubs/gazette

Dog & Kennel
Pet Publishing, Inc.
7-L Dundas Circle
Greensboro, NC 27407
Telephone: (336) 292-4272
Fax: (336) 292-4272
E-mail: zinfo@petpublishing.com
www.dogandkennel.com

Dog Fancy
Subscription Department
P.O. Box 53264
Boulder, CO 80322-3264
Telephone: (800) 365-4421
E-mail: barkback@dogfancy.com
www.dogfancy.com

Dogs Monthly
Ascot House
High Street, Ascot,
Berkshire SL5 7JG
United Kingdom
Telephone: 0870 730 8433
Fax: 0870 730 8431
E-mail: admin@rtc-associates.freeserve.co.uk
www.corsini.co.uk/dogsmonthly

WEBSITES

Dog-Play
www.dog-play.com/ethics.html
A cornucopia of information and pertinent links on responsible dog breeding.

The Dog Speaks
www.thedogspeaks.com
Canine Behaviorist Deb Duncan's site, filled with useful advice on canine etiquette, behavior problems, communication, and relevant links.

Petfinder
www.petfinder.org
Search shelters and rescue groups for adoptable pets.

INDEX

A

B

C

D

E

I

J

K

L

M

U

V

W

Y

ABOUT THE AUTHOR

Deborah Wood is one of America's most popular pet writers. She is the author of ten books, including *Little Dogs: Training Your Pint-Sized Companion* and *The Little Dogs' Beauty Book*. She is also the pet columnist for *The Oregonian* newspaper. Deborah has won many awards for her work, including twice being named "Newspaper Person of the Year" at the annual Dog Writers Association of America writing competition. She lives in Portland, Oregon, where she competes in obedience trials with her Papillons and volunteers with her therapy dog at a children's hospital.

Photo Credits

Paulette Braun: 9, 11, 85, 90, 104, 141, 149, 185, 189, 190
Carrieanne Larmore (Shutterstock): 152
Dwight Lyman (Shutterstock): 4
Tammy McAllister (Shutterstock): 96
pixshots (Shutterstock): 35
Chin Kit Sen: 132

All other photos courtesy of Isabelle Francais